Edith Augusta Sawyer

Mary Cameron

A Romance of Fisherman's Island

Edith Augusta Sawyer

Mary Cameron
A Romance of Fisherman's Island

ISBN/EAN: 9783744665254

Printed in Europe, USA, Canada, Australia, Japan

Cover: Foto ©Thomas Meinert / pixelio.de

More available books at **www.hansebooks.com**

MARY CAMERON

A Romance of Fisherman's Island

BY

EDITH A. SAWYER

With a Foreword by HARRIET PRESCOTT SPOFFORD

"Oh, is it not to widen man
Stretches the sea?"
— *Sidney Lanier*

BENJ. H. SANBORN & CO.

BOSTON, U. S. A
1899

PRESS OF SAMUEL USHER,
BOSTON, MASS.

To the Members

OF THE SAMOSET ISLAND ASSOCIATION, AND TO ALL WHO HAVE

SHARED IN THE HOSPITALITY OF THE ANNUAL MEETINGS

ON FISHERMAN'S ISLAND, THIS STORY, FOUNDED

LARGELY UPON HISTORICAL FACT,

IS DEDICATED.

A FOREWORD.

The coves and indents, the bays and river-mouths, along the coast of Maine, are a part of my earliest memories. All the lovely region seems to me still a sort of fairyland which, when a little child, was all my own. Through its bewildering waters I made repeated voyages, sitting on the deck of the packet-ship by day, tented by blue heaven, ringed about with blue sea; here, on dark nights, I was carried in sailors' arms down long wharves, rowed out upon the dim swell to the one light visible in an immense blackness, and handed up the gangway, trembling with awe at the unfamiliar greatness of the world; here, on bright lonesome mornings, I was rocked in the schooner *Girls* from reach to reach of the beautiful St. Croix; or on another day, when the swift *Huntress* could not make the Eastport wharf in the low tide and sudden tempest, we went ashore in boats to cross fields of wet seaweed, with the needles of the rain in our faces. I can still feel the cool salt breath there steal in from outer deeps, and see it draw a film across the stars. I can still hear the cry of the great winds, with storm upon their wings, sweeping in from reefs and ledges, singing their high death-song of wreck and drowning men. The rafts, the sun-soaked hulls and tarry ropes of the coasters, the light-houses, the islands — whose primeval pines stood like dark sentinels and whose sea-edges were fringed with tender green of dipping birch and willow — the elf-like sails flitting

5

here and there, the great ships taking sun and shadow and stealing away like grey ghosts, the gloom of cliff and steep, the rolling fogs pierced by a red flame of sunset, the vast tossing stretches of live sunshine and azure and foam, of rose and silver, of violet mists whose dim distances veiled a still farther and yet undiscovered country — all these remain in my recollection, clothed with an atmosphere, half dream, half reality, of vivid beauty, that makes the wild sea-region all to me that a land-locked Arcady or Tempe has been to the fancy of poets and singers from the early days to this.

Kind reader, may you find in the sweet, strong, fine story of *Mary Cameron*, set in the scenery of the coast of Maine, with its added wealth of humanity, of love and sorrow and joy, all of this gentle enchantment, too!

HARRIET PRESCOTT SPOFFORD.

Newburyport, Mass., June 1, 1899.

CONTENTS.

CHAP.		PAGE.
I.	FISHERMAN'S ISLAND	I
II.	THE FIRST ANNUAL MEETING	14
III.	INFLUENCES	23
IV.	WINTER ISOLATION	35
V.	SECOND VISIT OF ISLAND OWNERS	42
VI.	SUMMER DAYS	60
VII.	WIND AND WRECK	73
VIII.	"OUT OF THE DEEP"	89
IX.	UP MARCH HILL	92
X.	THE HEALING OF THE SEA	103
XI.	NEW SCENES FOR OLD	110
XII.	KNOWLEDGE AND FEELING	127
XIII.	AWAKENING	143
XIV.	"THE BEST IS YET TO BE"	161
XV.	MANIFOLD CHANGES	174
XVI.	HELP FROM MAN TO MAN	186
XVII.	"LOVE TOOK UP THE HARP OF LIFE"	191

MARY CAMERON:

A ROMANCE OF FISHERMAN'S ISLAND.

CHAPTER I.

"O, it's a snug little island!
A right little, tight little island!"
— *Thomas Dibden.*

THERE was a hush and stillness about the late July afternoon. The flood-tide came up against the rocks with a faint murmur. A motionless jellyfish floated in the clear water close to the shore. The sun, disappearing behind the trees on Southport Island, touched their tops with gold. Far away, homeward-bound fishing boats moved slowly along. Faint violet-gray clouds hung over the southern horizon ; above, the salmon-colored sky shaded to pale blue, growing into deep blue overhead. Across the still waters the air came with a soft sea fragrance.

The gold on the tree tops changed to bronze, then russet. The sails in the distance took on a yellow tinge. The sea color deepened into an exquisite blue,

1

with gleams of pale yellow. Just as the sun set, the red rays shone out from Ram Island lighthouse.

A tall, sinewy man stood on the Fisherman's Island wharf ready to catch the line from the in-coming cat-boat. His spare figure was sharply outlined against the somber gray rock behind. He wore high rubber boots drawn up over snuff-colored trousers, a yellow oil-skin jacket, and a black sou'easter; his rolled-back collar revealed a strong neck, and his pushed-up sleeves brought to view marvelously tattooed arms, on which the muscles stood out like cords. He was bronzed almost to copper color by exposure to sun, wind, and storm. The gray stubble of a close-cut beard left visible the square outline of his jaw and chin; a heavy gray moustache hung over his mouth. Scanty gray hair showed behind his ears and under his sou'-easter. A large nose, high cheek bones, shaggy eye-brows, under which were clear, keen, dark blue eyes — all marked a man of simple life and rugged force.

" Here we are, father, safe and sound ! " exclaimed the bright-faced girl who was holding the rudder while the tall, lithe skipper eased the boat along the wharf. " We 've had a splendid sail. I bought my new dress, and here 's a letter for you. Jack, you bring the bundles, all but my dress, I'll take that," she said, as she jumped out, the boat made fast. "Come on, father; what's in your letter?"

"Oh, that'll keep till we get to the house. Run along an' show Aunt Hetty your new gown; I expect she's as pertikelar to see it as you be to have her. I'll help Jack moor the boat."

"No, come now, dear daddy," insisted the girl; and he went.

The tide was out, leaving the little cove half bare. Great dark masses of seaweed covered the rocks below high-water mark, and gave a gruesome effect to the surrounding flats. The cliff, along which the path ran from the wharf to the house, rose abrupt and steep, of heavy rock with deep, lengthwise fissures at the wharf end, then sloped into a line of sand beach around the cove, just beyond which, on high ground, stood the little house, toned with nature's homely gray and russet.

There was something joyous, spring-like in the girl's figure as she walked on ahead, occasionally having to wait for her father; she stood tall, erect, like a young pine tree, as if she had all the elements of support in herself.

"Aunt Hetty's getting supper for us, sure as you live," she said; "there's smoke coming out of the chimney. She did n't need to, and she'll be cross as two sticks afterwards to pay for it."

"Hush, Mary, you must n't talk that way. Your aunt means all right."

"Yes, I know it," answered the girl, with quick compunction. "And I've brought her some calico for aprons; that will please her better than anything." She vanished into the house, leaving her father on the little front porch to read his letter.

Presently she came out, her hat off, her wind-tossed brown hair curling all around her face, and a large red apron tied over her blue flannel best dress, saying as she sat down and leaned against her father's knee, "I declare I'm tired. It was hard work waiting around Boothbay and buying things. And Aunt Hetty *is* cross; but she would n't let me stay and help. Who's your letter from?" Letters were great events on Fisherman's Island.

"Judge Weston. He's comin' here next week with two or three of the owners, an' mebbe their wives. Can't we give 'em a fish-chowder dinner?"

"Yes, I suppose so," said the girl thoughtfully.

"Aunt Hetty will help, I guess, and we can borrow her chairs and dishes."

"An' the judge says probably he an' Rob Weston 'll want to stay a day or two longer," went on the old captain; "you remember that nephew of his, don't you? Used to live over to Boothbay — that tall, yellow-haired fellow who always was makin' picters; he 's tryin' to get a livin' by it now."

Mary remembered. Rob Weston had been about five years ahead of her in the Boothbay schools. He had gone to live with Judge Weston after his parents died, and when he came back to visit he called her "Miss" Mary.

"I 'd just as soon the nephew warn't comin'," said Captain Cameron with a sidelong glance at his daughter. She was sitting by his side now, holding his big knotted hand in hers. "I don't like these city chaps."

When will a man learn that if he wants to keep anything from a woman he must not even think of it in her presence?

They sat there for a long time, planning about the visitors. There was no twilight. The moon, high in the east before the sun went down, had blended day and night.

"Ain't you ever comin' to get your supper?"
sounded a high pitched voice just behind them. "The
cream o' tartay biscuits' been done this five minutes,
an' I'm goin' home." Without waiting a reply, Aunt
Hetty turned, and with stiffly erect figure, stalked
grimly along the path to the smaller house near the
wharf, the skirt of her scant wrapper catching in at
her heels, a calico apron over her head.

Since the first of May the two Cameron families
had lived on Fisherman's Island, which lies out in
the open sea three miles "as the crow flies" southeast
from Boothbay Harbor, on the Maine coast — a long,
narrow island scantily wooded. The circumstances
of their coming here were somewhat out of the
ordinary.

The island had been bought by about a dozen
gentlemen — lawyers and prominent men — who the
previous summer, cruising along the Maine coast, had
liked the quaint barren island, found the property in
the market, and, forming an association, bought it
forthwith, electing as president Judge Levi Weston,
both in years and honor their senior member. That
winter, in the Maine legislature, where some of the
owners chanced to be serving their State's interests,

the association was incorporated as the "Samoset
Island Association of Boothbay," and a liberal charter
granted.   But, though legally "Samoset Island" now,
the name of "Fisherman's" has always clung to the
island.

Then the matter slipped from the minds of most of
the owners.

In April, however, Judge Weston bethought himself
of the approaching summer, and partly to get a breath
of good Maine air, partly carrying out a half-formed
project, went to Boothbay.

As the steamer *Lincoln* drew up to the wharf,
Judge Weston's eyes fell on David Cameron's wea-
ther-beaten figure.   "Just the man, yes," he told
himself

" I have come to see you, Cameron," he said, shaking hands heartily as he stepped from the gang plank.
"How has the world been using you?"

The two men had not met for several years.

"It's been a hard pull, Judge, a hard pull," the
other answered.

"Come up to the Boothbay House with me," said
the judge; and in his habitual manner, going at once
to the gist of the matter, he explained that he and his

friends had bought Fisherman's Island and wanted
somebody to live there to look after things. " Will
you go, Cameron?" he asked.

Captain Cameron knew the island well. Life would
be lonely and isolated there. But times were hard;
he had lost his best sailboat last season through the
carelessness of " rusticators " — as the native popula-
tion sometimes call the summer visitors — and the
winter's catch of fish had been small; besides, he was
growing too old for hard work now. " If Mary 'll go,
I will," he said finally, after they had talked the matter well over. " She's had a good bit of schoolin',
'bout all Boothbay gives, an' she's mostly content to
be 'long with her old father. I 'll come round an'
tell you in the mornin'."

After the supper dishes were washed that night,
Captain Cameron told Mary of Judge Weston's offer.
Brave girl that she was, and womanly, too, beyond her
eighteen years, she faced the prospect unflinchingly,
for she knew what a relief from money care the
change would bring to her father.

" We 'll go," he said, the next morning, hunting up
Judge Weston early. " Mary's the most superior girl
in Boothbay," he declared, with a burst of pride.

"She's got more sense in her little finger than a dozen other girls put together."

"She has good pluck, anyway," returned Judge Weston, "and that she ought to have, being your daughter," he added affectionately, for the two men had been boys together in the old town and had never lost touch with one another, widely different as their lives were.

"There's no reason why this should n't be a life-berth for you, if you want it," said Judge Weston. The two men had walked down to the wharf together, for Judge Weston had to take the morning boat. "The salary will come regularly, and you ought to get something out of the lobstering and fishing. I shall be down with some of the other owners this summer, and I have made a contract for a good wharf to be built on the north end of the island. You will have near neighbors in the lighthouse people on Ram Island." The *Lincoln* gave a final whistle. "Well, good-by, David."

"Good-by! God bless you, Judge," said Cameron. And the *Lincoln* was off.

The two Cameron brothers, David and Donald, had lived next-door neighbors in Boothbay all their married lives. Both were sea captains, and neither had been very successful, for competition runs high in the coastwise trade these days.

The odds had seemed especially against David. A few years before he had been obliged to abandon his schooner, which went ashore in a gale, and he had barely escaped with his life. Shortly after, his wife died. Broken by these misfortunes, he settled down to fishing and boat building, and kept a small yacht for pleasure parties.

Captain Donald Cameron still sailed the *Flying Kestrel*, and was away most of the time. It was often insinuated that he liked better going to sea than being in hot water at home, for his wife Mehitable — Aunt Hetty, as Mary called her — was one of the people who consider it their mission in life to keep others up to a high level of conduct by constant criticism.

"Why can't Jack and I go and live in the other house on the island?" Aunt Hetty demanded when she was told of the proposed change. "Mary needs lookin' after; Jack can keep on buildin' boats, and goodness knows how you'd ever manage out there all by yourselves, anyway. It ain't a very sightly place, but Jack's father ain't at home enough to have it matter where I live," she added, with a touch of bitterness. Her face showed that she had lost much of the song out of life.

There were evident advantages in having another family on the island, and David knew the good heart that lay behind Aunt Hetty's hasty tongue ; so he wrote for permission. It was granted, and the household goods of the two families were speedily moved into their new quarters.

The snug, natural harbor formed by the cove and the smooth tawny sand beach on the north of the island gave safe anchorage for their small fleet of boats. The two houses were almost within speaking distance of each other. Aunt Hetty and Jack settled themselves in the smaller one, close to the new wharf — a little box of a house.

The other, a plain wooden story-and-a-half house, more than a hundred years old, looked barren and uninviting indeed when Mary and her father entered it. Two moderate-sized rooms, one on each side of the tiny entry-way, and two rooms overhead, an ell kitchen and a shed, was the extent of the houseroom. But Mary's deft fingers did much to transform the place. The sunny kitchen was soon shining with care ;

leading off from it was the dining room, and here Mary had her sewing machine. Across the entry-way the best room held state, full of old furniture; a large cabinet was filled with curiosities and knickknacks from over the seas; on the walls hung two marine pictures, one of Captain Cameron's ship under full sail, the other of Hong Kong Harbor, a few samplers worked by Mary's mother, and a steel engraving of Abraham Lincoln, " one of the biggest men that ever lived," said Captain Cameron. There was no carpet, but an inheritance of braided rugs covered the floor.

With Jack's help, Mary took down the fireboard which covered the huge, high fireplace opening into the stout central chimney. On the left side an open cupboard built into the wall furnished a place for their odds and ends of rare old Eastern china, on the right was the delight of her heart, a " speak-a-bit" corner or ingle nook — the tradition had come down from remote Scottish ancestry — formed by a wooden settle which extended the short distance between the fireplace and the south window. The room had three windows — the north looking out over the sheltered cove harbor, the south toward Seguin, and the west over to Squirrel Island and Southport.

Mary held a housewarming in the best room, inviting the other family, one damp May evening after they were well settled. "I'm glad we are out here just by ourselves," said home-loving Jack as they sat around the soft blazing driftwood fire.

"Mary, it's dretful extravagant havin' this big fire," Aunt Hetty protested; "you'll burn a half a cord of wood every time."

"Never mind, Aunt Hetty," answered Mary gaily. "We've got the whole Atlantic Ocean for our woodpile."

CHAPTER II.

"There is no such thing as chance, and what seems to us
Merest accident, springs from the deepest source of
destiny."
— *Schiller.*

HOW many of those folks is comin', do you
s'pose?" Aunt Hetty's voice was pitched
higher than usual.

"Oh, six or eight," answered Mary, pausing from
her sweeping to look out of the western window,
"and I hope they're going to have a good day."

"I sh'd think they might have sent more notice,"
sniffed Aunt Hetty. "Serve 'em right if it did rain.
The almanik says look out for rain about this time."
She took the frying pan off the stove, and walked
with quick, nervous steps into the pantry. The
doughnuts, crisp and brown, were piled high in a pan.
Fresh loaves of bread and crocks of cookies filled the
pantry shelves.

"I'm pretty near beat out; here we've done nothing
but work, work, for three solid days, gettin' ready, and
now likely 's not it'll rain, and they can't come after
all, — more's the pity," she went on, inconsistently.

" You did n't need to help ; I could have got along without you," answered Mary. There was a touch of Scotch fire in her make-up, and she banged the kitchen door behind her.

" That niece of mine has been more trouble to me since her mother died than my Jack has all his life," Aunt Hetty invariably told her Boothbay friends. " I don't know why, but she never agrees with me. She's dretful headstrong. Young people nowadays is amazin' cocksure of everything." Yet Aunt Hetty devoted herself unsparingly to Mary, and she had taken hold with right good will in the preparations for the owners' visit.

It was about ten o'clock. The wind, easterly in the early morning, was shifting to southwest and the low mist rolling seaward.

" Aunt Hetty, quick ! Here's the steamer coming," cried Mary, running in from the front porch.

" This ain't no time to be dawdlin' round watchin' boats," replied Aunt Hetty grimly. " I've got to start the chowder goin', for I suppose they'll be most starved when they get here, like everybody else. There's a sight of work to be done."

Mary, disregarding the implied suggestion, hurried back to the porch.

"See if you can make out what boat it is," said Captain Cameron, handing the marine glasses to Jack, "your eyes are younger than mine." All three were watching.

"It's the *Samoset*," said Jack, who could name almost every craft on their ocean highway, miles off.

Mary disappeared to change her dress, and then set out for the wharf with her father, to meet the party. Jack vanished.

A sudden feeling of dismay seized the girl. These people, all but Judge Weston and Rob, were strangers; and Aunt Hetty had announced, "You've got to look out for the company; I ain't the lady of the house."

When Captain Cameron went down the sluiceway to help fend off the boat, Mary hung back, uncomfortably conscious that she was the target of many eyes. The heavy gray rocks behind the girl brought out in vivid relief her tall figure, which held a certain grace, though there was as yet little of the softening touch of maturity. On nearer view her face was attractive. The damp wind had ruffled her brown hair into clinging disarray, and her brown eyes looked out with a direct, appealing glance ; the sensitive mouth and firm, round chin showed determination and delicacy.

Captain Cameron's face glowed with genuine hospitality as Judge Weston introduced his companions. Mary stayed in the background, and felt more than ever like an awkward child when Judge Weston, leading her by the hand out before the entire company, said, " This is my godchild, Miss Mary Weston Cameron, the presiding genius of the island." Then he led the way with her to the house, past a delightful confusion of boats, lobster traps, and fishing gear. Last of all to step up on the little porch were a tall, well-built young man and the most beautiful girl, Mary thought, that she had ever seen. The man, whom Mary recognized instantly as Robert Weston, came up to her. "How do you do, Miss Mary? I remember you in Boothbay long ago. Let me introduce you to Miss Kendall."

The girl said something conventional, — her indefinable air of superiority seemed to stifle Mary, — then she joined the group who were seating themselves on the porch and the rocks around. Mary beat a hasty retreat to the kitchen.

" Your chowder 's ready," announced Captain Cameron, appearing at high noon round the side of the house, with a preliminary toot of his fish horn.

Mary, heated and flushed, helped serve the dinner. The hurry and strangeness of her position took her thoughts from herself. She caught entertaining snatches of conversation, and listened, wide-eyed, to the novelty of toasts. Dinner over, the island owners — there were five of them here, one, a man well known in the Senate of his country,— spent an hour in the quaint parlor, smoking and talking over plans for a clubhouse, while the ladies, glad to escape from the hot dining room, sat outside, listlessly waiting. Mary joined them shyly, forgetting that Aunt Hetty was toiling over the dishwashing; and she covertly noticed everything connected with these unknown people. What would n't she give if she could only sit there so calmly, gracefully, like Miss Kendall, taking part in the chance talk, and looking (she said to herself, passionately) " as I could n't look if I tried a hundred years."

Miss Kendall, who was evidently about Mary's own age, had dark eyes, a fair, clear complexion, and was daintily dressed from hat to shoes. The other girl, with yellow hair, frank gray eyes, and a well-built, strong-looking figure, was Miss Merrick, the picture of good health and easy good nature. Both girls seemed quiet; but Mary noticed that their faces brightened when the gentlemen joined the group.

"Now those of you who are good walkers would better climb that hill and get a look at Monhegan Island and Pemaquid, then come back round by way of the south shore," said Judge Weston, seating himself in an old straight-backed, flag-bottomed chair. "I 'm too heavy and too short of breath for much walking. Miss Mary will show you the way. You go, too, Mrs. Sargent; I will take care of little Katharine." And the party started off, leaving the five-year-old girl perched on Judge Weston's knee, listening with big round eyes to the story of the old Indian king Samoset, who used to cruise around the island in a black boat on dark nights.

Mary, bareheaded, led the way up the winding path, past the boathouse and clumps of tall raspberry bushes. Rob Weston kept close pace with her, admiring with his artist's eye her lithe, elastic motion, for long climbing over the rocks had made her as graceful and sure-footed as a deer. "I must sketch that girl sometime," he said enthusiastically to Miss Kendall, falling behind for a moment. Eyes shining, cheeks reddened with the exercise, hair wind-tumbled, Mary made a suggestive picture as she stood on the little pile of stones that marked the summit of the island. Miss Kendall did not like her any the better for it.

From the summit to the south shore was a good twenty minute walk. Bordered with golden-rod and white elder blossoms, the path ran along by the marsh over the ridge to the bar, where Mary told them the sea swept across in rough weather, making two islands of the one — on over the rocky pasture end, until they came to the steep white rocks, the air freshening ever, the noise of the sea beating down their voices. Monhegan Island lay forty miles to the left, Damariscove a few miles ahead, and Seguin well off to the southwest — all set in the brimming, exulting sea.

"Every breath you draw has a cool, invigorating core to it," said Senator Kendall gratefully. He had not been long away from stifling Washington.

But there was only time for a glance at the broad panorama, for Mary, as her quick ear caught a far-away whistle, exclaimed, "There comes the boat for you," and they turned regretfully back.

On their return walk Miss Kendall tried to draw Mary into conversation. "What can you possibly find to do out here on this lonely island?" she asked, with languid interest.

"Plenty, every day," was Mary's laconic, loyal reply. Ill at ease, self-conscious in the presence of these two city girls, she now only wanted them to be gone; she was not like them. Drawn by an instinctive sympathy, however, she fell behind with Mrs. Sargent, who showed so kind an interest that Mary was led to talk freely about herself; her heart warmed, too, toward Mr. Loring — John, the old judge called him — who shook hands cordially when he bade her good-by, and said, "You have helped give us a happy day, which I shall always remember."

"If you 've carried off some of the island's sand in your shoes you 'll be comin' back again; it 's a sure sign," was Captain Cameron's farewell.

"Aye, aye, Captain, we 'll come many a time," said Senator Kendall, standing, hat off, at the boat's stern.

Judge Weston and Rob remained. Supper was a rather silent meal. Jack had not come in from hauling lobster traps, Aunt Hetty was out of sorts and spoke only to ask their wants, and Rob Weston ate with a ravenous appetite. Captain Cameron and Judge Weston talked spasmodically of the locality of Pentecost Harbor, where, according to Rosier's narrative, "the ship of Captain George Weymouth, the Archangel, lay at her moorings May 30, 1605, under an island in the capacious and newly discovered haven." Judge Weston was disposed to think the "island" Fisherman's, the "haven" Boothbay Harbor.

Supper over, Mary started Aunt Hetty homeward. "Poor, tired Aunt Hetty," she said to herself reproachfully. Then she washed and set away the supper dishes, put some bread to rise, and crept off to bed, miserably out of peace with herself and all the world.

Down on the rocks by the water's edge, Rob Weston was dreaming dreams of his art and seeing visions of the future. He liked the sense of the great overarching sky, the glinting stars, the untamed ocean wearing itself restlessly against the rocks, each force bounded by itself, pouring all its power into its own mighty life.

CHAPTER III.

"Speak a speech that no man knoweth,
Tree that sigheth, wind that bloweth,
Wave that floweth."
— *William Watson.*

THE limpid sea lay like an unclouded mirror the next morning. Rob was out and up on the island hilltop soon after breakfast to get the glory of the morning light into his mind. But after a few moments Mary, from the kitchen window, saw him plunging with long strides down the hill. Out he came where she was washing dishes, his blue eyes shining, his thick, tawny-yellow hair rumpled from his haste.

"Come on, Miss Mary, let's go for a row around the island while it's calm."

"But I've got all my morning work to do," she answered, the rich color rising into her face.

"Oh, never mind! I'll help; it won't take us long." And he whisked an apron from its peg, tied it around his waist, and helped in such a boyish, bothering fashion that Mary, in self-defense as the last dish was dried, said, "There, I'll go now, but let's hurry off, for if Aunt Hetty sees me she will find some reason for my staying at home."

Mary's own boat, a trim little craft, painted green below and blue above the water line — to match the sea and the sky, she explained — was moored off the old pier on the point. She jumped in first, pulled the boat out by the stern line, unfastened it, and was putting the oars in place when Rob brought the boat in by the painter, stepped in, and taking possession of the oars said, " At least you 'll let me do the rowing."

" Why, yes, if you want to." Mary's cheeks crimsoned. She had done something wrong, judging by his tone.

Rob's long, steady strokes sent the boat swiftly through the narrow channel on the north, separating Fisherman's from Ram Island, that little rocky spot where the lighthouse clung. The point rounded, he let the boat drift with the outgoing tide. The water was indescribably clear; looking into depths, he could see shells and barnacle-studded rocks on the sandy bottom twenty feet below.

Mary made no effort to talk. She was looking seaward now, and Rob Weston was looking at her. The soft brown tam o' shanter cap which she wore deepened the color in her eyes, her hair gleamed with warm lights, and her brown blouse waist helped make a harmony so complete that Rob vowed mentally to sketch her that afternoon "if she'll let me." She was not like other girls he knew.

"These are the Hypocrites," she said, suddenly rousing herself as Rob rowed into one of the narrow channels between the long ridges of white rock to the east of the island. "Years ago a sea captain ran his brig ashore here. He thought he was in deep water, and that the white he saw away ahead was a sand beach; so he afterwards named the rocks 'Hypocrites.'"

A few clouds were in sight now, and curling tremors of wind broke the serenity of the sea. When they rounded the south shore, choppy waves were dashing against the shelving white rocks. The boat began to toss violently, yielding to the great living pulse of the sea. They were dangerously near the long lines of reef. Mary sat very quiet, with the habit of one accustomed to boats. Rob threw off his cap, set himself square at the work, and rowed around the point without their taking in a drop of water. He had been on the 'Varsity crew in college, and as he sat there opposite her, erect, flushed, victorious, it was her turn to look at him.

The glimmering purple-green color of the sea, the shifting clouds with their stir of life, absorbed Rob into the impersonal condition common to the artist nature, and woke, too, the touch of melancholy never far away. Forgetting Mary, he was saying softly to himself : —

> "Break, break, break,
>   On thy cold gray stones, O Sea,
> And I would that my tongue could utter
>   The thoughts that arise in me! "

"That is from Tennyson, is n't it?" asked Mary shyly.

" Yes ; what do you know about Tennyson?" came the confusing question.

" Oh, I read his poems sometimes."

" What else do you read?" There was distinct condescension in Rob's tone.

" Whatever comes my way," was her short answer. And he could get nothing more than "yes " or " no " from her.

" Do you read much?"

" Yes."

" Do you like living here?"

" Yes." She would not have said " no."

" Better than Boothbay?"

" No," reluctantly.

" Do you like nature — birds and such things?"

" Yes."

Rob gave it up as hopeless; in fact, pulling along the rough western shore against the tide was enough to occupy his attention. Every now and then he stole a glance at her as she sat there, immovable, petulant, her mouth compressed into a straight red line, her beautiful hair blowing about her face. " She's a stubborn little thing," he said to himself.

When they reached the wharf he helped her out with a great show of gallantry, saying, " I 'll see to fastening the boat." She seemed relieved to let him, and hurried off to the house.

Her mood changed at dinner, — a scanty meal that suffered because of her absence, — and she talked excitedly of her flowers, the sea gulls, fishhawks, and her tame squirrels. She wore her new dress, which Aunt Hetty had made, — a bright plaid, with broad lines of red, blue, green, and yellow.

" Heavens! what a gown!" said Rob to himself.

"Why hadn't I sketched her in that old brown rig this morning? I can't get her now!"

While Mary was hastily cooking the fish dinner, Rob, out in the boathouse, had made friends with Jack, and the two had agreed to go gunning. Jack was a fine-faced lad of sixteen, with the far-away look of the sea in his blue eyes; a goodly youth, sun-browned, strong, straight, and supple of limb.

Crack! crack! came the sound of their guns all the long afternoon. Judge Weston had been looking over law papers during the morning; now, his after-dinner pipe smoked, he was peacefully napping in Mary's cushioned "speak-a-bit" corner. Captain Cameron was off fishing. Aunt Hetty had kept away from the house all day. Mary wandered about restlessly.

When the sun's rays began to slant across the island, the two sportsmen came home down over the hill. Mary ran out to meet them. "What luck did you have?" she asked eagerly.

She saw in a moment. There was a magnificent great sea gull, its white breast torn and stained, two beautiful herons with drooping heads, and one of her gray squirrels.

"You dreadful, dreadful man to kill my squirrel!" she blazed at him, her face afire. "How could you! O Jack, why did you let him!"

"Why, Miss Mary, I did n't know it was yours," Rob said with real distress. In the zest of the shooting he had forgotten Mary's story of the squirrels, and seeing a good shot, although he was not out for such small game, he had brought it down.

"They 're all mine," she said, darting a defiant glance at him, "and it 's just because I 've tamed them that they did n't keep out of your way." (Small credit to my aim, thought Rob.) "It 's all Jack's fault; he ought to have told you," she went on with quick justice.

"I — I did n't think you 'd mind just one," said Jack lamely.

"Of course I do, you cowardly thing." Her anger was breaking out again, and she ran into the house, too proud to show any more feeling.

Later, she slipped over to Aunt Hetty's. "You must come to supper," she insisted. And Aunt Hetty was quite ready to forego her solitude. Jack talked boats with Rob. Judge Weston praised the clam stew and Mary's cooking, but she sat sullen, unresponsive. The old man glanced at her keenly from time to time.

Nineteen years ago that spring, when visiting Boothbay, Judge Weston learned that a baby daughter had come to David Cameron's home, and he had asked to be godfather, with the privilege of naming the child Mary for his mother. Ever since, even in his busy existence, he had kept in touch with her young life. As a baby, Mary wound her arms about his neck, holding him with all her tiny strength when it was time for him to go. She had grown shy in the last years, for she seldom saw him, but he was continually glorified in her young imagination.

There was many a charming side to this man's life. He was a literary Bohemian, and in his bachelor quarters on —— Street, in Boston, there were rare old volumes — old friends with whom he loved to commune. He had many idiosyncrasies, which a comfortable inheritance and a good law practice in the past enabled him to indulge; and his personality was picturesque. His bristling, bushy eyebrows and dark, piercing eyes ornamented a fine head set on a rather heavy, thick-set frame. In movement he was slow, and in dress careless. His hats were a noticeable feature of his dress

— a Panama straw in summer and a broad-brimmed beaver in winter. His wit bubbled luminously, and his cheerful ready smile made one feel always welcome. Of an ardent and impulsive temperament, he was fond of people, and felt life keenly. Yet he had the calm philosophy of content; others might do the fretting and the worrying. His was the philosophy that cultivates the humanities and encourages the amenities of life, that helps lift the feet of the weary and lighten the load of the afflicted.

As he sat smoking on the porch that evening in the glowing twilight, the kind old man called Mary to him, and began talking about life. Much that he said ran counter to the girl's world of ideals, for she was singularly childlike in her knowledge of life; but she entered into every situation with singular intelligence and sympathy, having almost invariably the right instinct. Then he turned the conversation to herself. He had observed her closely these last two days, and the instincts of fatherhood are strong in thoughtful men.

"It is character that counts in this world, after all, Mary. You must be true to your best self, the best you can learn from people, from books, from the

Bible. Study and learn and observe all you can.
You will not always live here, cut off from the world,
though there is many a girl who would be glad of such
a comfortable home."

" How can I learn anything out here?" asked Mary
with a discontented sigh.

" Your father has a fair education, for he has kept
his eyes open going about the world ; he can help you,
and you can help Jack. When you have a chance,
notice how young ladies like Miss Kendall and Miss
Merrick carry themselves." Mary made inward protest.

" Try to be always bright and happy," he went on,
for he had noted her latent tendency to morbidness.
" Learn to make your own sunshine. A man likes to
come home to a sunshiny woman ; it helps him to the
brave attitude of life that Robert Louis Stevenson
writes about. It's a lonely life at best for a man or
a woman, without the anchor of a home — lonelier for
a man, because a woman makes a home wherever she
hangs up her stocking bag. And what it means to a
man to come home at night to a cheerful, sunny
woman, only he knows who has had to fight the hard
battle of life alone."

The judge stopped talking. Mary moved nearer,

and timidly put her hand in his. There is a silence between friends that is more eloquent than words.

Ram Island light was sending its mild red rays over the neighboring waters. The quiet waves lapped against the rocks with a soothing murmur. Overhead the watchful stars seemed to bend nearer, and the air was full of the subtle fragrance of the sea.

Rob appeared in the doorway. "Uncle Levi, you'll be getting rheumatism out here," he remonstrated, "and you know we must start out early tomorrow."

Judge Weston roused himself from his reverie and went in, first shaking hands warmly with Mary.

"Wait a minute, will you, Miss Mary," said Rob. "I'm awfully sorry that I shot your squirrel. I can't bring him back to life, but Jack has promised to get him stuffed for me over at Boothbay. Will you keep the squirrel, and remember to forgive me?"

His earnest voice, the deference of his manner, made longer resentment impossible, sore as Mary's heart was. And she answered with a break in her voice that he found bewitching, "I know you did n't mean to do it. I will keep him to remember you by."

She held out her hand in token of forgiveness as

she turned to go into the house.   He took it with such a close, lingering pressure that she was glad the darkness hid her suddenly burning cheeks.

The two guests were off to Boothbay early the next morning, to connect with the Bath steamboat for Boston.   Why did the day seem so cheerless all at once to Mary as she watched the vanishing figures?

CHAPTER IV.

"In youth, beside the lonely sea,
Visions and voices came to me."
— *Thomas Bailey Aldrich.*

AFTER winter fairly set in, the Fisherman's Island people found life, the mere living of it, quite as much as they could manage, thrown so entirely as they were upon their own resources. The weather became the matter of first importance — as happens always with people living in isolated places; the changes of the sky and sea, the flitting of coasting vessels to and fro, the visits of the sea fowl, sunrise and sunset, the changing moon, the northern lights, the wheeling constellations, made up the outward events of the days and weeks.

Mary had faced the thought of the winter, with its solitude, bravely, but the finer balanced mind loses elasticity and stagnates in such extreme isolation. Aunt Hetty kept bustlingly busy from morn till night, doing her daily housework with infinite care and scrupulousness, then using the short afternoon daylight for sewing and the long evenings to knit stockings or

work on carpet rags. Captain Cameron and Jack
went the rounds of their hundred or more lobster pots
every morning, except in severest weather, and afternoons worked in the boat shop, where Captain Cameron was building a stout dory, and Jack remodeling
his catboat the *Kady*.

The winter came hardest on Mary. Their little
house seemed almost to take care of itself. She
was too vigorous-natured to sit contentedly sewing
seams or knitting all day long; there were no
visitors to come and no places for her to go save
to see Aunt Hetty, or occasionally, on fair, still
days, to Boothbay with her father or Jack on their
weekly trips for supplies. Once in a while Jack
spared time to take her over to spend a half day on
Ram Island.

So she turned to reading everything that fell into
her hands — the papers that Judge Weston sent each
week, the books, indifferently chosen, which the lighthouse tender left at Ram Island once a month, and
over and over again the books which Rob Weston had
left — novels of the Duchess and the Rider Haggard
type — summer reading, as one says, mainly of the
kind to stir the imagination and awaken an unnatural,

distorted sense of realities. She read in her own especial corner, too, recklessly building roaring fires in the
great fireplace. Aunt Hetty grumbled when she saw
the fresh smoke curl up from the other house chimney
nearly every afternoon.

"I declare for it, David Cameron, the way you fetch
an' carry for that girl makes my own back ache,"
Aunt Hetty remonstrated with her brother-in-law.

But he invariably answered, "Mary shall have her
fire just as she wants it, even if I have to go over to
the main for wood. It's about her only pleasure."

Once in a while the strain of the loneliness grew
too great to endure in silence. To Mary's passionate
complaint, "I wish something, anything, would happen," Aunt Hetty, self-centered, unimaginative, replied : —

"I call that temptin' Providence. I don't see why
anybody should complain when she's got work enough
to do an' a roof over her head an' enough to eat."

Then repentant, remorseful, after she went home,
the girl would rush back to Aunt Hetty and beg her
never, never to tell her father that she was lonely.

So the winter wore away, and Mary learned the
beginning of that lesson of renunciation whose chap-

ters we must study one by one, until the lesson of
greater gain is grafted in peace upon our hearts.

Spring comes slowly along the Maine coast, and
nature does not thoroughly rouse herself until well
into April. Mary's spirits woke with the season.
She scoured the house from top to bottom until everything shone, then settled herself cheerfully to the
slow task of making over her last year's dresses, with
Aunt Hetty's help. She would rather have been out
of doors where the sprouting grass, the budding
trees, and the birds seemed to call her continually.
Sometimes she and Jack ran races the length of the
island. As the days grew warmer, she planted flower
seeds in every available spot near the house, and fell
into the habit of taking long walks over the island.
Nature seemed to answer her moods, and she was
better content with the island life.

All through the winter and spring the two families
talked of the owners' coming in the summer. It was
early in July, however, before any message arrived.

" Only three members of the association can come this
year," wrote Judge Weston, " Mr. Sargent, Mr. Loring, and myself. Rob Weston is coming with me, and
Mrs. Sargent is to bring Miss Kendall. Expect us

the first Wednesday in August for a fish-chowder
dinner. Rob and I will stay over night, if you can
keep us."

It was the evening before the appointed day. Mary
was sitting out late on the little porch, her tired mind
working incoherently. To-morrow she would see
Rob Weston — Miss Kendall, too. All during the
long winter she had been endowing Rob with the
virtues, the vigor, the comeliness combined in every
hero of every book she had read, and she had pictured again and again her meeting with him.

It takes only a slight reality to make a hook for a
woman to hang an ideal upon, and Mary Cameron was
no exception; rather, indeed, the isolation of her life,
the untried depths of her nature, but added strength
to the hook and adornment to the ideal.

"Mary!" called Captain Cameron from the kitchen,
where he sat reading his Bible, "you'd better come
in; it's getting damp, and it's time you was goin'
to bed."

Captain Cameron was a devout man. Years ago,
as he honestly told now, he had led a wild, hard life.
When he was forty years old he married a Boothbay
school-teacher — all conscience and love, from whom

Mary inherited much of her temperament — who thought she could regenerate the stalwart, high-tempered young sea captain. But it was not until two happy years before Mrs. Cameron died that the change came.

Nowadays every Sunday the old man went in sunshine and in storm, too, whenever possible, to the morning service at St. Anne's, in Boothbay, the Episcopal chapel where his wife had been a steadfast worker. Then in the afternoons — his cold lunch eaten, or having taken dinner with some old friend — he conducted a mission Sunday-school class for the Boothbay young men, in an old storeroom near the wharves, where chance sailors could drop in.

He read nothing but religious newspapers and his Bible, — Mary and Jack, from their reading, told him what was going on in the world, — and every night he held family prayers in the little kitchen — trustful endings to homely days. There was always an earnest, patient prayer, " That it may please thee, in thy mercy, O Lord, to bring back my boy Edwin, and forgive me for driving him away from home in the days of my sinfulness," — for his only son Edwin, eight years Mary's senior, had, in a passion of anger over palpable injustice from his father, run away to sea ten years ago, and never been heard from by any sign or trace.

Captain Cameron's simple human faith of his latter days, born out of much tribulation, absorbed his mind and gave peculiar tone to all his utterances. His inheritance, from a Scotch grandfather, of firm energy of will, and his wide acquaintance through his former roving life with all sorts and conditions of men, saved him from weak fluctuations of purpose and despondency, and saved him, too, from leading that dual life common to elderly men of the rigid New England type, whose spiritual fervor finds no channels through their daily lives. Even Aunt Hetty said of him, "I'm one of the folks that like to watch your Sunday Christians between Sundays; but you don't need to watch David Cameron."

To-night when they rose from their knees, Mary put her arms impetuously around her father's neck. "I'm so happy here with you, father. Don't let's go away, ever!" and she burst out crying.

"Why, Mary! you're all nerved up. Come, come, go to bed," said her father, kissing her with more than usual tenderness.

said mentally, "and how refreshing after so many conventional girls!" Mr. Loring was no longer very young.

Soon Rob Weston was listening, too, to Miss Kendall's chagrin. Then the conversation grew general, and Mary found to her disappointment that they had engaged Captain McKown from Mouse Island to cruise around with them in his catboat that afternoon to see the local yacht race.

"Do come with us," urged Mrs. Sargent.

"We should be so glad to have you," chimed in Miss Kendall with cool civility.

Mary wanted to go, but with feminine unreason said, "No, I have too much to do."

They hurried through with the fish-chowder dinner — over which Mary had taken pathetic pains — and went outdoors again, the ladies with Rob to watch the beginning of the races, the owners to continue their dinner discussion of plans for a clubhouse. Mr. Sargent, who had built many houses, had rapidly sketched a plan.

"Sakes alive!" exclaimed Aunt Hetty, watching them from the kitchen window as they walked out to the knoll to the westward, "they'll never put up a clubhouse out here. Those lawyer folks is always talkin', talkin'."

"I am sorry you won't change your mind and come with us," said Mrs. Sargent, as she and Mr. Loring bade Mary good-by before starting for the boat. "We must send some books to that girl, John," she added later; "she has a good mind, I know, and it needs better food."

Rob Weston walked down to the wharf with Miss Kendall. There was a careless ease about his tall figure in its brown golf suit, an indefinable rhythm about the girl, which made them seem well adapted to one another, to Mary's wistful eyes. When the party was fairly off she was furious with herself for not having gone. But her pride rankled yet because Rob Weston had not urged her going; why, he himself hardly knew.

Toward sunset the Mouse Island boat headed for the island to leave Judge Weston, Rob, and Jack. It had been a sultry afternoon, long and lonely to Mary, who had alternately helped Aunt Hetty and watched the races through the marine glasses, keeping the catboat in sight. As the boat approached, Captain Cameron said, "We'd better go over to the

wharf an' bid the folks good-by again." Father and
daughter were out on the porch.

" No, I'm not going. I hate that Miss Kendall,"
said Mary, bitterly.

" Why, Mary! what nonsense you're talkin'." There
was mild astonishment in Captain Cameron's voice.

" I don't care; she makes fun of me. I can feel
it," said the girl. And Captain Cameron humored
her; he did not always understand Mary.

Rob Weston, with Jack, reached the house ahead of
Judge Weston and Captain Cameron. " Sorry you
did n't go with us, Miss Mary," said Rob. " It
was n't exactly rough, but there was a heavy swell on,
and the ladies did n't sail very well. I suppose you
are a good sailor."

" The rougher it is and the bigger the swell, the
better Mary likes it," put in Jack loyally. " It's
some fun to take her sailing. Say, Mary, we're
going to have a rousing driftwood fire down here on
the rocks after supper."

" Yes, Miss Mary," Rob interrupted, " Jack says
there is plenty of wood out on that rocky beach back
of the house. I am glad I gave up that dance at the
Squirrel Inn this evening."

How the hungry men enjoyed the hot steamed-clam supper which Mary served with such a suddenly brightened face! The Sargents, with Miss Kendall, were making Squirrel Island their headquarters.

"Oh, hang the supper dishes! Just leave them," said Rob in answer to Mary's protest against starting the fire at once.

"All right," said Mary, catching his impatient mood. "Maybe Aunt Hetty 'll come over and do them."

Mary slipped away to change the blue flannel dress skirt and white shirt waist in which she had looked so well that day, for the old brown blouse and a short brown skirt — infinitely more artistic to Rob Weston's observant eye. From the beach to the spot chosen for the fire was a three minute walk, and Mary persisted in carrying her share of the wood.

"There must be terrific winds to drive this beach back so far," commented Rob, coming across a ridge of wave-worn pebbles in the grass. "Is n't living on this island dangerous in rough weather?"

"Yes; when it blows hard we have to put a leeboard down to keep the island from drifting away," retorted Mary gaily. "Even Monhegan Island sways in a gale."

A feeling of good comradeship was springing up between them. "Don't take that great log alone," she exclaimed. "I 'll help carry it."

"The Tempest" and Miranda flashed into Rob's mind. "So you 'll help me bear the log awhile," he said, his dark blue eyes sending a keen glance at her. This was growing interesting.

But the allusion was lost on Mary. Together they carried the heavy log to the rocks down on the shore, a hundred yards from the house. Jack was fetching and carrying with the utmost willingness, the spell of Rob's personality upon him, for Robert Weston had the dominating power which results from a cold nature and an intuition bordering on the feminine.

"Now we 'll have a scientific fire," said Rob, arranging corner logs and cross sticks over a pile of shavings, with layers of broken spar, bones of ships, and general wreckage.

The flames burst out gloriously. In a trice the fire was crackling and blazing, with the sound and color which only a driftwood fire can show, in its apparent struggle to give forth again the awful energies, the lurid pictures, which the mute wood has witnessed.

The sea was bumping at regular intervals on the

rocks below. "That rote means a storm comin' within the next three days," said Captain Cameron. Wrapped in a coat, he sat leaning against the rocks, toasting his feet, for August nights, even after warm days, are cool on the Maine coast. Judge Weston, growing rheumatic with advancing years, dared not risk exposure in the evening air.

After his exertion Rob stretched himself on a shelving rock. Mary, aglow with excitement, — a witching vision in the firelight, — flitted about, now prodding the fire with a long pole, now darting off into the darkness to reappear with long festoons of dry seaweed, which crackled and snapped in the flames. "I wish I were a savage," she exclaimed on one of her returns, "then I could live out of doors. I'd like to go off hunting up to Moosehead Lake or off on a whaling voyage sometime. I don't see why girls shouldn't go, just as well as men. Jack, you must take me."

"It's just as you say, Mary," answered Jack. He always kept up with Mary.

"If I'd been a savage I should have been a fire worshipper." Mary suddenly whisked back as the fantastic tongues of flame, many colored, leaped high toward her. "Come on, Jack, let's have a fire dance." And she seized the astonished youth, dragging him breathless in a sudden mad whirl three times around the fire.

" Mary! Mary!" called her father, amazed.

"Mary Cameron! ain't you ashamed to be carryin' on so!" Aunt Hetty's voice seemed to come out of the darkness, made more intense by the bright firelight. "I declare, how you do act!" she said. Mary, suddenly subdued, sank down on the bank near her father. "Here you went gallivantin' off an' left your supper dishes, an' I 've just this minute finished 'em for you, an' now you 're out here, actin' like the witch of Endor."

Fortunately for Mary, another arrival turned the attention from her — save that Rob was thinking to himself, "What did that old woman come and stop her for?"

The dip of oars drew nearer, then ceased. " It 's Sam Merrill," called back Jack. He had run down to the water's edge, and soon returned with the lighthouse keeper from Ram Island, who scrambled readily over the rocks with his wooden leg.

" He is spryer than any two men," was commonly

said of " Sam," as everybody called him. He had lost his leg in the lighthouse service on Seguin Island and had later been given charge of Ram Island, a fourth-class light, requiring less care.

" I see your fire a-goin' an' could n't stay home," said Sam, " so I told my woman I 'd got to get over an' see Cap'n Cameron 'bout some lobster pots. I know it did n't fool her one mite, but I had to have some excuse, an' she 's allers good-natured, after all. Glad to meet you, sir, glad to meet you; kindly hope you 're well," he said, when he was introduced to Rob. Then he talked a few moments with Captain Cameron about the lobster pots to satisfy the New England conscience, of which he was in full possession.

" See here, Sam, won't you tell our fortunes," asked Mary, " if you 've got your cards here? "

" Stuff and nonsense," sniffed Aunt Hetty. " Your fortune 'll come fast enough without pryin' into the future."

But Sam was already pulling out of his jacket pocket a pack of well-worn cards. " Got 'em here, sure enough," he said.

" Tell Mr. Weston's first." Mary's voice came out of the shadows.

"No, yours, Miss Mary," insisted Rob; he wanted to see her nearer in the firelight.

"Make your wish an' cut with your left hand," directed Sam impressively, after he had shuffled the cards. "An' keep the wish in your mind all the while."

Mary came forward close to the fire, near where Sam had seated himself. She cut the cards almost solemnly. Sam had only once before told her fortune, and his reputation ran high.

Mumbling some mysterious words, Sam told off certain cards. These he spread out on a flat rock and began : —

"There ain't much in this fortune, but what there is is queer, kinder. Here's something like a long lane that ain't got no turnin' yet awhile; I 'spect that's livin' on the island. Things all goes one way, kinder sad like, an' dretful feelin'. You set your heart on somethin', an' mebbe you get it an' mebbe you don't. Seems as if eddication or book larnin' or somethin' stands in the way. There's a heap o' money comin', an' presents, an' letters."

"Stuff and nonsense, Sam Merrill!" interrupted Aunt Hetty. "You tell just the same things to everybody."

" Is that all?" asked Mary.

" Yes, 'bout all; guess I ain't feelin' like it to-night," replied Sam, with a deprecatory glance at Aunt Hetty.

Rob, spellbound, was watching Mary. Her hair, loosened with the dancing, had fallen waving around her face; her cheeks were brilliant, her eyes flashing, her breath coming quick and fast. " I'd make my fortune if I could paint her now," he said to himself. "Is n't she going to get married?" he asked with sudden whim.

" Yes, oh, yes, some day; but the course o' true love ain't goin' to run very smooth with her," Sam answered glibly. "Now it's your turn, Mr. Weston," he added, shuffling the cards again.

" My! but you 're goin' to have adventures, heaps of 'em. An' here's a dark lady an' a light com-plected lady, an' things kinder mixed up together." And Sam rambled on, Mary listening, all attention, Rob indifferently, till Sam said, " It 'pears to me you 're goin' to make a new beginnin'."

" That interests me," said Rob. " What is it?" he asked, half credulously.

" Somethin 's goin' to happen new an' different,"

said Sam, delighted to have made a hit. "You're goin' somewheres an' goin' to make a heap o' money."

"More likely spend a heap," said Rob. "You were all off in that nonsense about the girls; I've never cared for anybody yet," — this was for Mary's benefit — "but it's rather strange about the other, for there is a change coming in my life. I'm going to Europe this fall to study art for three years."

Mary rose so suddenly that some of Sam's cards fell into the fire. One thought was whirling through her brain: Europe was as far away as another world, and three years a lifetime!

Sam rescued what cards he could. "I have a pack here which I'll leave for you," said Rob, puzzling over Mary's start.

"It's high time we was goin' into the house, Mary, an' endin' this nonsense," put in Aunt Hetty. "I for one can't stay out any longer, an' it ain't proper for you to," she added bluntly. Her instinct was as quick as her tongue. Captain Cameron had left when the fortune-telling began. He was liberal as regards others but inexorable with himself, and cards had helped make havoc with his early life.

"Good night," said Sam, hurrying off. He was

afraid of Aunt Hetty and wanted to go before he was sent. Jack went to help him start; they were firm friends for many a good turn done one another.

"I'm waitin' for you, Mary," said Aunt Hetty, pointedly. Mary had seized an old fish pole and was absently poking the fire, fast dying now. "That fire's all right to leave."

"We will come right along," said Rob, but Aunt Hetty seated herself grimly to wait. Rob spread the ashes over the glowing embers, trying to get a word with Mary meanwhile. But not a word would she speak, until, dropping the pole, she turned to Aunt Hetty. "I'm ready now." And she walked in silence to the house, Rob close behind her.

From the quaint parlor, where he stopped for a bedtime smoke with his uncle, Rob Weston heard Captain Cameron's voice in the kitchen and guessed what was going on.

Captain Cameron noticed that Mary did not respond to the prayers that night.

The lights were soon out in the little house. Outside, Seguin, Ram Island, and Burnt Island lights made long reflections across the water, and the crescent moon glimmered through a bank of low clouds in the west.

CHAPTER VI.

" What then meant that summer's day
Silence spent in one long gaze? "
                            — *Robert Browning.*

YOU 'D better have breakfast with us; it will bring the roses back to your cheeks," said Judge Weston, with kindly insistence, the next morning; for Mary, after pouring the coffee, rose from the table saying, " Father and I had breakfast an hour ago."

Her face had color enough in a moment. "Thank you, I can't stay; I have some work to do." And she vanished into the kitchen.

But Rob did not intend her to be let alone. He hurriedly ate his breakfast and followed her.

" Miss Mary, will you put on that brown blouse, and let me sketch you out by those big rocks behind the house?" He leaned against the door near the table, where Mary was filling lamps. The turned-back sleeves of her blue shirt waist showed her firm, white arms. As she was about to use her scissors he took them, obliging her to look at him. Then he bent his pleading eyes upon her. " Possibly your picture will help make my fortune in Paris."

Both her vanity and her sympathy were touched, and Rob was triumphant over the hesitating " Yes." " Come now," he begged, " the light is just right."

Disregarding Aunt Hetty's probable comment, Mary, with sudden elation of spirits, ran upstairs to change her dress.

A sleepless night had left her with a pallor which gave deepened delicacy to her face. " Jove! she'd be tremendous if you once got her well roused," thought Rob.

He seated his model against the gray-brown rocks, with their brilliant background of blue sky, — Mary first examining, with childlike curiosity, his paint box, palette, and tubes of color, — and stationing himself at due distance, began his work.

Stiff and conscious at the outset, she spoiled his expectation. But gradually the tension wore off, her figure relaxed, and seeing him steadily at work — he was only putting in details, the yellow-green grass, the gray lichened rock — she lost herself in a popular novel he had given her; after awhile the book dropped from her hand, and she looked out over the sea with

just the expression of strained wistfulness he had
hoped to catch. Occasionally her eyes met his, and
met an absorbed look — the man was lost in the artist.

The sitting lasted almost three hours. In her
abandonment Mary forgot the cramped position, the
physical discomfort. Suddenly Aunt Hetty's voice
broke the stillness.

" Mary, I sh'd think 't was time you was gettin'
dinner! Here it is after 'leven o'clock, an' your
father's brought in a cod he 's just caught. I 've biled
some lobsters for you ; I s'posed you 'd forget to."

" Confound the woman!" muttered Rob under his
breath. Mary swayed insecurely when she rose.
"I 'm afraid it has tired you, Miss Mary!" he exclaimed contritely. "I can work now without you,
and perhaps you 'll sit again some time ; I 'll be putting
in the color of your dress." And he dipped a fresh
brush in the burnt umber on his palette.

Mary gave a hurried glance at the canvas in passing. "Do I look like that?" she asked herself, color-
ing with pleasure as she walked away.

An intense excitement dominated her. She wanted
to grasp the moments. It did not seem to be herself
who was moving, thinking, speaking. She could not

have explained it, — a young girl does not analyze emotion; she simply feels it.

At dinner the talk turned on Rob's going to Europe.

"I wish he had taken something besides painting pictures for his life work," said Judge Weston; "but it's been in him all his life, and I want him to do the best he can. A man's work must be more than a pastime. Yet even talent is mediocrity in Paris, where hundreds of artists are trying to express the inexpressible, and to grasp the unattainable. But the experience will show what stuff there is in him, at all events."

"Paris ain't the place I sh'd chose for a young man." Captain Cameron knew whereof he spoke. "There's always two sides to a question though, an' your nephew's a grown man now. He'll probably come out all right. I 'spect the worst thing it'll do will be to knock the religion out of him."

"Jack says I can take the *Kady* to sail over to Inner Heron Island this afternoon," Rob announced, to change the subject. "Will you come with me, Miss Mary? I have to call on an old friend who's staying at the Madockawanda House."

" Yes, I'd like to go." Mary's answer came in a low voice.

Captain Cameron looked up. " I s'pose you know all about boats," he said ; " there ain't much wind, though, an' like 's not you 'll get beca'med comin' back. Do you think you 'd better go, Mary ? "

" Oh, yes ! dear daddy, please ! " said Mary, with a beseeching look. Captain Cameron made no further protest.

Before the two started Judge Weston took Rob aside. " Be careful, Rob " ; his tone was significant. " I think too much of Mary Cameron to have you trifle with her."

The *Kady's* sail caught the wind as soon as she was out from the lee of the land. Jack, watching the boat from the hilltop, repented bitterly having offered her to Rob. Rob had not once suggested his going, too.

As they passed out north of Fisherman's Island, lazy seals, sunning themselves, slipped off from the rocks into the water, barking like young dogs. Over the sparkling sea white gulls were flying in low circles, and above the surface, schools of young mackerel flecked their shining sides. Past the Ocean Point shores on the west, and across Linnekin's Bay, the southwest wind sped them rapidly, and the *Kady* cut through the water "with a bone in her teeth."

"I'm going to whistle for more wind," exclaimed Mary. She was standing against the mast, her hat off, her hair tossed by the wind. "I notice breezes come better for lively tunes than they do for hymns," and she whistled "Nancy Lee" in a way which Rob found bewitching.

Easily moved, impressionable, Robert Weston had always followed his impulses hither and thither, save that he held unswervingly to his art. School and college had given him only such teaching as he chose to take. His nature was so ingenuous, so magnetic, that people unconsciously bent to him. The one strong affection of his life was for his uncle, whose bounty had been unlimited. Their common feeling of loyal appreciation for Judge Weston formed a definite bond between Rob and Mary, affording a background of interest.

Mary stopped whistling, her thought going back to what Judge Weston had said about being like other girls.

"What do men like best in a girl?" came the unexpected question, as she sat down and put on the brown tam o' shanter cap. The expression in her eyes baffled Rob.

" Sympathy," he answered after a moment. Then he returned the question.

" What does a girl like best in a man?"

She colored close up to the waving hair. " Oh — she likes to be cared for, I suppose," she stammered.

" Yes, that's just it," Rob went on ; he was at home in *fin de siècle* discussion. " A girl's heart is moved by little things that never affect us. Now I like a girl who is sympathetic, so that you can always count on it, and yet who is different at times, — like the ocean, you know, always the same underneath, with a lot of variety on the surface."

Mary's heart sank. Sympathy she could feel, even if she could not express it, but variety — she could only be herself.

They were close to Inner Heron Island now, for the two mile run had taken hardly half an hour. Rob made the landing and moored the boat, leaving the sail set to shade Mary. " I 'll be gone only a few minutes," he said as he went up the wharf steps.

Mary, deep in thought, was drawing her hands back and forth through the water when Rob returned.

He scowled at two young fellows who were staring down from the wharf at Mary, unbeknown to her, and hurried the boat off.

Even in the short time since Rob landed, the wind had died away perceptibly. They drifted out, scarcely making headway at first. The sky was a luminous, unruffled blue and the sea a succession of long, lazy swells.

Rob talked a little about Paris. The old lady friend had been giving him motherly advice. " I think I shall be happy with three whole years for my art," he said; " but after all, the wrench of going away makes me wonder if I could n't do just as well at home. Still, a man has to keep up with the procession these days, or else fall out."

" I wish I had lived a hundred years ago;" Mary spoke impetuously. "Men and women were truer and better then. I don't like the books that are written now; they don't seem real."

" The trouble is they are too real," said Rob.

" Perhaps," Mary replied, " but I don't understand them. I love to take life hard, don't you, and not have it just make believe? I 'd rather feel things, and have them almost kill me. It 's a satisfaction; you can hug it to you." She drew her arms close to herself.

Rob did not answer. Speech began to seem needless this golden afternoon. He shifted the sail and headed the *Kady* out to sea on a long tack, to get the good of the wind. The air was heavy with soft fragrance ; the waves, lapping against the boat, made faint music. The light glowed in a shining haze as the sun sank lower, and the water gleamed exquisitely iridescent.

When the *Kady* at last drifted out opposite Fisherman's, Rob turned her prow westward.

" It 's almost six o'clock ! " he exclaimed, glancing at his watch.

The sun had told the time to Mary, but when Rob said, " We shall get back sooner if I row," she answered, " The tide will take us soon enough."

Straight before them now lay the pathway of gold. As they sailed toward the sunset, the level rays of reddening light fell full on the girl's face, touching it into rare beauty. Rob looked at her half bewildered. Was it all real?

The sun vanished beneath red billows of cloud back of Southport. Above these clouds the sky color melted from soft green into delicate deepening blue. The half-moon, warm and red, hung in midheaven, and the evening star looked out, red-warm, too.

"I don't believe Mars is inhabited, do you?" Mary's voice had a far-away sound. "The Bible does n't say so."

"But it does n't say, either, that there are n't other worlds as well as this," answered Rob. It seemed natural enough to be talking about such things with this girl.

"Why should n't there be a Bible for this world, and another for some other world?" Mary went on, musingly. "If God can do everything, there need n't be any limit to worlds and peoples. But just think of the millions of stars! It is like a great weight over-head."

Rob moved nearer her, as if protectingly; and he saw a look in her eyes that responded to something rising in his own heart. He was fast forgetting Europe, his plans, his uncle, everything save the witchery of time and place.

"Before you go, I want to ask you something," she said, with clear, shining eyes.

"Ask me now."

" No, not now."

" Why not? "

" Oh, I can't yet," she answered, looking away.

Rob Weston prided himself on his worldly readiness, but here he was strangely at a loss. This girl was both fire and ice, now so near, then in a moment as far away as the stars.

They were approaching the Fisherman's shores, all too soon, Rob thought. Monhegan and Pemaquid lights shone in the distance, the fog-bell on the Hypocrites sounded faintly. Ahead, the red light streamed out from Ram Island, as Rob turned the *Kady* into the narrow channel between the two islands.

" I 'll take the sail down," he said, as it began to flap under the lee of Fisherman's. He gave the rudder over to her. " They 'll know we are coming," he added, as the sail creaked along the mast.

" How late is it? " inquired Mary.

" About eight o'clock. Will your aunt mind? " he asked, coming aft.

" Yes," said Mary with a sigh.

" I 'm awfully sorry." He was close to her. Her shapely brown hands, not beautiful, but homelike, were on the rudder, and he put his own upon them.

After a brief, bewildering moment, she quickly thrust her hands behind her, and moved away in a tumult of new feelings, saying passionately, " You have no right to do that."

" I could n't help it," he said in a low tone, springing to save the *Kady* from scraping against the wharf.

In a moment Jack appeared, followed by his mother. Once landed, escaping from Aunt Hetty's sharp comments, Mary hurried toward the house. Rob overtook her.

"Tell me now what you wanted to ask me," he begged.

" No, don't ask me now ! "

" Will you before I go ? "

" Yes; to-morrow." She ran away from him into the house, and kept close to her father the rest of the evening. He and Judge Weston were talking over old school days.

The next morning a heavy gray fog shrouded everything ; lifting fitfully at intervals, it showed an angry, tossing sea, then the curtain shut the island again into a silent wilderness, save when the fog-signal sounded from the Cuckcolds, or the bell-buoy on the Hypocrites broke the stillness.

" If you 've got to go, Judge," said Captain Cameron at breakfast, " we must be off right away, for we 'll have to feel our way over to the main ; Jack's got his boat all ready."

" Why not stay another day ? " suggested Rob.

" No, I must be off." Judge Weston's tone was decided ; the dampness had given him a twinge of rheumatism. " Besides, we 're likely to have a spell of weather out of this, Captain Cameron says."

" Yes, when the sun comes up double, same 's it did yesterday, look out for weather," explained Captain Cameron. " Sorry to have you go, but the wind has hauled 'round to the nor'east, an' we 're in for a storm."

" Come into the other room a moment," Rob said to Mary, as they all rose from the table ; and she followed him.

There was something pathetic in the droop of her figure, as she stood by the table in her " speak-a-bit " corner, and it roused his manhood ; he felt a momentary mad desire to take her in his arms. But the flush of the evening had gone : it was cold daylight now. His manner stiffened, though his eyes kindled.

"What did you want to ask me?" His tone was very gentle.

She waited a moment to gain control of her voice. "Have you — have you ever been confirmed?"

"What!" The amazement in his voice was unmistakable.

"Have you ever been confirmed, in the church?" She repeated the question, her voice still lower.

"Oh, yes, years ago. But I don't make much of those things. Why do you ask me?" How the light tone hurt her!

"Oh, never mind," came the embarrassed reply, as she turned away.

"Rob! Rob! hurry up!" Judge Weston called peremptorily.

"Just a minute, Uncle Levi," Rob answered impatiently. Mary was going toward the door. He stopped her in front of the fireplace. "Give me those flowers, will you?"

She took the sweet pease from her belt. He seized the trembling hand with the flowers.

"Will you write to me while I am away?" he asked in an uncertain voice.

"Yes." He could not see her face.

"Good-by — Mary! I shall never forget these days here." Bending over, he kissed her forehead and rushed from the room.

The others were waiting outside the house. There was strong will in the girl. She summoned all her self-control and went down to the beach, where Jack was ready with his dory to take them aboard the *Kady*.

"Is the luggage all in?" asked Judge Weston.

"Aye, aye, sir," answered Captain Cameron, "picter an' all."

"Well, good-by, Mrs. Cameron," said Judge Weston, shaking hands with Aunt Hetty. "Good-by, Mary," laying his hand affectionately on her shoulder, "we shall meet again sometime." His kind, keen eyes looked deep into hers.

Rob was the last one to step into the boat. "Good-by, once more," he said to Mary.

A moment later the fog shut the boat from sight.

"What you goin' to do now?" asked Aunt Hetty, detaining Mary. "I 've got to go to cookin'. It 's a dretful nuisance, this havin' folks come an' hinder your work."

"Pick some raspberries," Mary answered at random. The thought of going into the house choked her.

"What, this wet mornin', an' leave all your work! I sh'd think you 'd lost your senses. You look 'bout fit to go to bed." Aunt Hetty gave the girl a searching glance. Mary turned and left her; she could not speak another word.

On she went, vanishing into the fog, past the house, past the great rocks looming ghost-like where Rob had painted her picture — only yesterday was it? — along the footpath to the narrow, rocky bar. There she threw herself down on the hard beach, a hundred fiery thoughts darting through her brain with intolerable torture. "Oh, if I could only die!" she gasped, tearless, shivering sobs shaking her from head to foot.

Was this the end of the dream in which she had lived all the long months since last summer? Rob had asked her to write to him, but oh, that interminable distance, those endless years!

The fish hawks shrieked overhead, the sea broke angrily on the rocks below, and the cold fog shut her in closer to utter loneliness.

She was very young, scarcely twenty, younger far in many ways than most girls, and all the untried tenderness and strength of her nature had gone into this dream.

Only the year before she had been admitted into the church, and to her sensitive nature, drawn by her father's influence toward things unseen, this had been the very opening of heaven. Yesterday, throughout that long summer day, the thought of separation, and a dread foreboding — never far absent from those who live where men go down to the sea in ships — had roused an unquenchable desire to know that Rob, too, would be in that high heaven. But when she asked the question, how little he understood! Even if she had explained, would it have meant anything to him?

Had she shown him how much she cared? Why else did he kiss her? Her pride rose to rebuke her and the sense of humiliation made her writhe in agony, till the last reaction from the strain of the past days came in choking sobs, which left her weak and exhausted.

The gulls whirled near, the great seas shivered and broke at her feet. Splashing drops of rain roused her. Was it late? She could not tell. Wet, chilled, wretched, she went slowly back to the house to make ready for her father's home-coming.

CHAPTER VII.

" Every day brings a ship,
  Every ship brings a word;
  Well for those who have no fear,
  Looking seaward well assured
  That the word the vessel brings
  Is the word they wish to hear."
  — *Ralph Waldo Emerson.*

ROB WESTON, looking out over gay, glittering Paris, chewed the end of his pen meditatively several moments before beginning his first letter to Mary Cameron. The ocean voyage had brought Fisherman's Island into his foreground again; it had retreated somewhat during the weeks of preparation.

The unfinished sketch upon his studio wall caught his eye. Paris and Fisherman's Island! Could there be a greater contrast? But what to say! " I can't make love to her," he exclaimed, " so I'll just pitch in and write as I would to anybody. She's such a sympathetic soul, she will understand." So he began writing.

" No. —, Rue de la Sorbonne,
  Paris, October 10, 189–.
" *Dear Miss Mary,* — Much as you were in my mind, I could not write in those hurried days before I

sailed. Being on the ocean seemed almost to bring
you nearer, though each puff of the steamer took me
farther away from you.

" Late September is a hard time at sea, and there
is n't much more to say about the voyage than that
I met a man from Bridgewater, Mass., an art student,
bound for Paris, too, a quiet, talented fellow, — good
ballast for me, — and we have cast in our lot together.
We reached Paris three days ago, hunted up a studio
the first thing, and are now almost settled in three
rooms near the Sorbonne, the Latin part of Paris,
where all the students live. We use the kitchen for
wardrobe and storeroom, take our meals at a café,
have our beds in the parlor, and are going to live,
generally, in the studio.

" The first day we went to the Louvre and saw
hundreds of famous pictures — I can't begin to tell
you about them — and dozens of art students, men
and women, young and old, sorry-appearing objects,
mostly, looking as though hunger and empty pockets
were near neighbors. I wonder if I shall come to
that! After we had looked at pictures until we
could n't take in another one, we went to Notre Dame
Cathedral, which at first is disappointing; but it
grows on me and makes me think of Victor Hugo's
stories.

" All the Parisian world has come back to town,
and it is a gay, stirring world. Sometimes it stifles

me, and toward night I would give a good deal to be
back at home, drudging away. We have splendid big
windows in our studio; the sunset view now is superb.
You ought to see it, — Eiffel Tower with a generous
sprinkling of hotel roofs in the foreground, to the
right Notre Dame, with St. Sulpice and others thrown
in, and on the left, the rest of this side of the Seine,
— all lighted up with a glorious, golden color.

"I expect to begin work at the Julienne Academy
next week. Meanwhile I am doing a sketch now and
then, and looking around. Already I have met half
a dozen men I know. I shall be very much occupied
with work and club matters, but that will not prevent
my writing often, and wanting to hear from you:
Your letters will be more than welcome, — I am impatient for the first one.

Ever most faithfully,
Robert Weston."

Summer, and the better part of autumn, too, was
now past. Mary's flowers had perished in the heavy
frosts, and the grass had faded to dull brown.
The shivering stacks of cornstalks, the cawing of
hungry crows, the shrill shrieks of sea gulls gave an
atmosphere of melancholy to Fisherman's Island.
All the summer cottages on Ocean Point and on the
neighboring islands were closed.

The wild geese had already wheeled overhead, southward bound, and Jack one day reported a white Arctic owl hovering around, — "signs of a long, cold winter," worried Aunt Hetty; she always went more than halfway to meet misfortune. Donald Cameron had been at home in September, and was now on his way to South America. He liked living at home on Fisherman's Island even less than in Boothbay.

Mary sat by the dining room window, waiting for her father, who had just sailed into the cove. The light from the setting sun reflected pale yellow streaks in the water near the shore; the wind, whistling, rattled the windows. A year ago, despite the cold, the girl would have run down to meet her father.

"Bhrr! but it's a bitter spell!" exclaimed Captain Cameron, opening the kitchen door. "I hope my little housekeeper's got somethin' pipin' hot for her old daddy's supper."

"Yes, a clam stew," said Mary, her face brightening as she helped the stiff hands untie the woolen comforter.

"Here's a letter for you," — Captain Cameron drew a thin, rustling envelope from his pea-jacket pocket, —

" an' it's got the first foreign stamp I've seen in many a year. I expect it's from that Rob Weston."

"Yes." Mary felt an odd tightening in her throat. She had almost given up the hope of hearing from him. She looked eagerly at the letter, postmarked "Paris, 5e 11 Oct., '9—." "I'll read it by and by; you must have supper now." But she found time to read the letter twice while her father put his heavy rubber boots into the shed, and brought the wood for the night.

She waited for him to ask about the letter after supper, but he settled down by the kitchen fire to read his papers, first handing out to her from the big market basket a firmly tied, plainly addressed package.

"More books, I do believe! Yes," said Mary delightedly, as she brought to light a volume of Shakespeare, a copy of "Lorna Doone," and several magazines. Another bundle of books had reached her in September, from Mrs. Sargent the two families decided by the Newton, Mass., postmark; and though the writing was unmistakably that of a man, Mary had written to thank Mrs. Sargent.

As she lingered late over the books, the girl began framing her answer to Rob Weston's letter, which, each time she read it anew, seemed to lack something, she hardly knew what.

With the autumn had come an introspective withdrawing into herself, new to Mary; the tide of self-analysis, sounding so persistently on the shores of the closing century, reached even to this remote island. Dazed and dejected at first, her questioning had grown gradually, aided by Rob Weston's silence, until she had come into a half-hearted determination to let the dream go. But it was touched into reality again by his letter, unsatisfactory though this was.

She copied and recopied her answer until every spark of naturalness was worn away. Then, trusting no one else to mail it, she sailed over to the mainland with her father and posted it herself.

Winter began with November. "I declare for it," said Aunt Hetty, "seems as if everything outdoors was dead set against us, all the winds of God an' all the frost an' cold."

Day after day Captain Cameron and Jack came in stiff and half frozen from hauling their lobster traps, — the Portland packet called once a month to take all the catch they had on hand.

Every morning, regardless of the weather, Mary

wrapped herself in an old coat of her father's, tucked her rebellious hair under the worn tam o' shanter, and went to see Aunt Hetty. Occasionally the two families talked of living together in the larger house, but Aunt Hetty always ended the discussion with, "I'm used to my own ways, and 't would fret me to have anybody else botherin' around the work; besides, livin' apart gives us somewheres to go." On Sunday afternoons she and Jack came to see Mary and stayed to supper; afterwards they all spent the evening in " the fore room," as Aunt Hetty called it, by the driftwood fire, while Mary read aloud. There was seldom a Sunday now when Captain Cameron could venture over to church, and it grieved him sorely.

A second letter came from Rob Weston, two weeks after the first one. Sam Merrill brought it early one morning — he had been to Boothbay the day before.

It was a short, impetuous letter, evidently written under the spur of strong feeling. Rob complained of the dreariness of Paris, the lack of comfort in his way of living, the loneliness of being among strangers, and he ended by saying : —

" I will tell you what I have not told any one else — that I am almost sure of having some illustration work

to do for the *Century Magazine*, which will take me
home early in the spring. Please do not mention this,
for many reasons."

A tumult of hope sprang up in Mary's heart, as the
long vista of three years reduced itself to a few
months, and she went about her work singing so joyously that her father, coming in to look over the
papers Sam had brought, exclaimed, " Why, bless my
heart, Mary! It does me good to hear you singin'
again." Aunt Hetty, too, noticed a change and commented to herself, "Girls nowadays do beat all; I
never saw anybody with so many ups and downs as
Mary."

That evening the girl wrote her answer, impulsively,
without copying this time; of course he did not like
that wicked, lonely Paris, — she hoped he would
surely come home, —she wished it were even sooner.

There had been an off-shore wind for two days, and
the sea was rolling into the cove in great toppling
green waves.

" David Cameron, I wish you'd forbid Jack goin'
to Boothbay!" Aunt Hetty burst into the kitchen
the next morning, a small shawl pinned over her
head, and a heavier shawl over her shoulders. Breath-

less with hurry and excitement, she sank into a chair, and the head shawl slipped back. She was short in stature, thin featured, with snapping brown eyes; her iron-gray hair, drawn tightly back, was twisted into a determined knot. "He says he's goin', an' I say it ain't a fit day."

"Well, it does look pretty squally," said Captain Cameron. "What's he goin' for? I mean to get over to the main myself, Saturday." This was Wednesday.

"Says he's got to have some spruce knees for the boat he's buildin'; but that's only an excuse, I know. He's possessed to start; I never saw him so set," answered Aunt Hetty, rocking nervously back and forth.

Mary kept on with her bread-making, her back turned to Aunt Hetty.

"I can't forbid his goin' if he won't stay for you, Mehitable." There was no mistaking Captain Cameron's tone, and when he said "Mehitable" Aunt Hetty was always silenced. Fastening her shawls closer, she started homeward, not much comforted by Captain Cameron's "Don't worry, Hetty, Jack knows most as much about boats as any man on the coast."

While the talk was going on, Mary's face burned scarlet. The afternoon before, she had found Jack in the boathouse, praised his progress on the new boat, and inquired of him, in an offhand manner : —

"When are you going to Boothbay again? I have an important letter I want mailed, — but please don't say anything about it."

Next to his boats, Jack loved Mary ; and without thinking much about the letter, replied : —

"I'll go in the morning; I must go anyway." Mary's interest gave him new zeal for his work.

His mother's objections were unavailing ; he only shut his mouth the closer, and told himself, "When Jack Cameron says he'll do a thing, Jack Cameron will do it." Accordingly, about ten o'clock, with Mary's letter in his pocket, he slid the *Kady* out from her moorings, and double-reefing the sail, started off on a long tack to windward. His mother's mind was somewhat relieved to see Sam Merrill set out, a few moments later, in the lighthouse cutter.

The two boats were soon running neck to neck. When they had vanished around Ocean Point, Aunt Hetty took her knitting, and went over to Mary's. "I'm that fidgety I can't stay alone," she said.

After the early dinner, she began looking for the *Kady*.

One o'clock struck from the tall, old-fashioned time-keeper in the kitchen corner. Its slow measuring of the hours suited Fisherman's Island; Judge Weston had often noted that.

The wind was coming heavy and squally.

Two o'clock struck.

"It's time he was in sight," said Aunt Hetty, clicking her knitting needles faster. From the window where she sat, she could see ominous bunches of cloud, racing southward.

The half hour sounded.

Mary moved around the kitchen restlessly.

"There he is now!" exclaimed Aunt Hetty with a sigh of relief, reaching for the marine glasses, as a sail came into sight this side of Tumbler Island. "Yes, it's the *Kady;* and, thank the Lord, there's Sam Merrill's boat too!"

Mary was looking eagerly over Aunt Hetty's shoulder; she had kept her growing anxiety to herself. The wind was raking the sea roughly, in great gusts.

Then, even then, while they both looked, the *Kady* veered, went down, vanished, was blotted out before their eyes!

Aunt Hetty's voice rang through the house with a shriek Mary never forgot. Like a flash the girl ran to the door and blew the horn to call her father. Aunt Hetty, after that despairing cry, with dumb anguish buried her face in her hands on the table.

Seizing the marine glasses, Mary looked strainingly toward Ocean Point. Each moment seemed an hour, and one of those hours that count for years in a life-time. She saw Sam Merrill crowd on more sail, run his boat swiftly to the spot where the *Kady* went down, and luff up into the wind; there seemed to be a struggle, then the lighthouse boat righted and headed homeward.

Captain Cameron heard the story. "Start up the fire, Mary," he said, hurrying off to the wharf. Controlling her own terror, Mary tried to comfort Aunt Hetty, who did not speak, did not even look up when the girl insisted that Jack might have been saved.

The strong northwest wind brought the staunch cutter, all sail set, into the cove like a flash. Ocean Point was only a mile distant.

"He *is* saved! They're bringing him!" cried Mary.

Aunt Hetty roused herself and stood upright, clutching the table, her face set, ready for the worst.

Slowly the two men came, carrying Jack — Jack, whose bounding step had left the house only a few hours before.

" There 's life in him yet," said Sam. They placed the limp figure on the old lounge, and began stripping the clothing from the unconscious body.

" Yes, his heart beats "; Captain Cameron was bending to listen.

It seemed that the cold of the numbed body could never be overcome. They rubbed until arms ached and hope almost died. Not a word passed Aunt Hetty's lips, but she fought like grim death for her boy's life.

Sam told the story, a few words at a time.

" You see, I was runnin' off to the westward, an' did n't get so much of that perticular squall, but I had to handle the cutter lively, I tell you. Then I looked out for Jack, an' there was the peak of the *Kady* just goin' under ! I tell you, the cold sweat stood out all over me. I see Jack's head in the water, an' I h'isted my jib in a jiffy, an' set over to him. Then 't was nip an' tuck if I could get him in, but as luck had it, the wind held up a bit, an' I luffed the cutter up into it, brought her 'round, watched my chance, an' made a

grab at him.   He was pretty nigh beat out, but he had
life enough left to help get himself in — he 'd had holt
of one o' them boat knees that drifted off.   Then he
just collapsed, went over in a heap.   I clapped my
coat over him, resked keepin' the sails all set, an'
headed for home."

At last Jack stirred, opened his eyes, shut them,
opened them again, and tried to raise himself, only to
fall back, half swooning, as he asked, "Where am
I — and where 's the *Kady?*"

While Aunt Hetty sat by her son, after he had revived again and fallen into a heavy sleep, Sam finished
his story.

"I know Jack must 'a had the sheet in his hand, he
would n't 'a made it fast in such a wind ; but I reckon
it caught on a block when he let it go.   There 's fifteen
fathom of water out there, an' the *Kady* must have
gone to the bottom like a streak, 'cause there warn't a
sign o' her when I got there 'cept a few pieces of wood
floatin' 'round."

Immediately on waking, Jack asked again, "Where 's
the *Kady?*"

"She 's foundered, Jack ; gone plumb down."   Sam's
voice was full of sympathy.

Jack put his hands over his face and turned to the wall. After a while, to rouse him, Captain Cameron asked, "You did n't have your sheet fast, did you?"

"Of course not, in that wind." Jack showed a flushed, indignant face. "I had it free, but when I brought the rudder round, the sheet caught on something, a block, I suppose, and the first thing I knew I was in the water, and the *Kady* was going down, — yes, I remember, she went down under my very eyes."

"Just what I told 'em; I knew you was too good a sailor to make the mistake of fastenin' your sheet," said Sam, soothingly.

Jack had been in the icy water over ten minutes, and his system, young and vigorous as it was, recovered very slowly from the shock. But though his strength came back, his energy did not. He had worked over the *Kady* until he knew every board and every nail in her, and the loss of the boat seemed to sap his life. Day after day he sat listlessly all the morning, often all the afternoon, at Mary's kitchen window, leaning back in the old stuffed rocking-chair, and looking out at the spot where the *Kady* went down; he could see the place best from here. His blue eyes had a dull, preoccupied look, he lost his ruddy color, and his hands grew thin and yellow.

Aunt Hetty stayed alone at home. "I can't bear to go with Jack, miserable as I am away from him," she told Mary one day, with a dry sob in her voice.

Day by day Mary grew more remorseful. "Jack would n't have gone, would n't have lost the *Kady*, if I had n't asked him to go," she reproached herself continually. One day he refused to eat any dinner; and that afternoon, Mary, seeing him so thin and wistful, burst out crying. Jack looked up in astonishment. She lifted her beseeching brown eyes full of tears: "O Jack, Jack! I can't bear to see you so wretched. It's all my fault for letting you go that day. I'm going to tell Aunt Hetty so."

Jack's eyes kindled with something of the old life: "I was going anyway, Mary, to get those boat knees; don't ever think of telling my mother I went for you."

CHAPTER VIII.

" ———— When old ocean roars
  And heaves huge surges to the trembling shores;
  The groaning banks are burst with bellowing sound,
  The rocks remurmur and the deeps rebound."
                                        — *The Iliad.*

IT was the last short day of the old year, — a day
to remember those at sea, and to be thankful that
you are safe on shore.

"Go and bring Aunt Hetty to supper," Mary had
begged her father; "Jack says he'd rather stay
here."

Captain Cameron came along the worn footpath
ahead of Aunt Hetty to keep the buffeting wind from
her. The waves were leaping high across the cove,
from ledge to wharf. "Guess 't was lucky I put
extra moorin's on the boats," he said, "an' I don't
know 's they'll stand it now."

There was a momentous weight of silence in the
gray air, a temporary lull in the wild wind, which had
shrieked all day in fury, after a week of raw, cold
fog. The dry, brown-crusted earth, caked and hard,
showed icy splinters of frost. Early in the day,

dozens of fishing vessels fled into Boothbay Harbor, but not a boat ventured out. Toward night the Boston-bound Bangor steamer put into Boothbay, an unprecedented thing.

"We must celebrate New Year's eve," said Mary, after supper, "and have a fire in the other room." Of late she had abandoned the best room. Jack liked better to sit by the kitchen window, and Captain Cameron, with the habit of simple-lived men, preferred the kitchen fire in the evening. The old man was rather feeble this winter — "getting old and rusty," he said — and it was harder for him to keep the wood pile replenished; Mary, noticing this, had the more willingly foregone her fires.

"My! those flames make my flesh creep; it's just like they was hissin' and groanin' over the wickedness they 've seen committed," said Aunt Hetty, with a burst of imagination, as the wood flashed forth green and blue and copper-colored flames.

Jack sat moodily looking into the fire, and Aunt Hetty gave herself up to being dismal. "No, I don't want to hear any stories, real or make-believe," she answered, when Mary suggested reading Dickens' "Christmas Carol" or that her father tell sea stories.

Finally, finding her attempts to enliven the little party of no avail, Mary said, " We may as well go back to the kitchen," for the rising wind flung shrifts of smoke into their faces and blew the ashes over the room.

Aunt Hetty, with a hesitancy new to her, delayed going home. " Guess I 'll take a look at the weather," she said about eight o'clock. As she put her head out of the door, a burst of sleety rain dashed into her face, and a gust of wind whirled through the room. She hastily closed the door.

" Don't let's go home," entreated Jack.

"Stay all night," urged Mary.

" I don't believe we could get home now," Aunt Hetty admitted reluctantly.

" By the looks of things, we ain't any of us likely to take much rest this night," said Captain Cameron ; " it's goin' to be a regular Tan-toaster."

Never since they came to the island had the elements racked them with such fury. The waves lifted up their voices, the island shook, the wind screamed and moaned at doors and windows, and at last beat out the fire.

Toward midnight the storm lashed itself into

greater force. Forks of lightning illumined the darkness, and the face of the sea in those flashes — black, swollen, angry — was awful to behold.

"Will the house go, David?" gasped Aunt Hetty, terrified with the might of the wind.

"No, Mehitable; it's built upon a strong rock foundation," answered Captain Cameron steadily. Tempests were as nought to him.

They were sitting, wrapped in coats and shawls, around the table, waiting, not for the passing of the old year, not for daylight yet, not for the ceasing of the storm; but waiting with the endurance learned from living by the sea.

Then the sleety snow began; hissing, lashing against the windows, it broke two panes of glass. Instantly the wind blew out the light.

Mary hastily stuffed her shawl into the gap, and Captain Cameron sprang to light the old horn lantern. Aunt Hetty wrung her hands mutely.

The clock from the corner began sounding the close of the old year.

Captain Cameron put the lantern upon the table, and, taking down his worn Bible from the shelf behind the stove, opened it and read the Psalm beginning,

"Out of the deep have I cried unto thee, O Lord"; then, falling upon his knees, he prayed aloud for all those in peril on the sea, for all wanderers on the face of the earth, for themselves, that they might find their peace in the new year.

Jack moved nearer his mother and put his hand in hers; his father was out at sea.

Captain Cameron replaced the Bible on the shelf, and, after trying ineffectually to light the fire, seated himself on the lounge to wait again.

"Lie down, father dear," said Mary. He yielded; and after covering him tenderly with an old great-coat, she drew her chair close to his side.

The old man's thoughts came back from his son, away now these ten years, to his daughter, whose waving hair, catching the light from the lantern, seemed the only other bright spot in the room.

Despite the stark storm outside, there was peace in that little kitchen.

They moved occasionally, through the long night watches, to shake off the numbing cold. Almost the only sound in the room came from the clock's ticking, or the sudden flare of the lantern.

At length the gray dawn, stealing in, roused them.

The world outside was covered with snow, deep and close-packed.

Captain Cameron found he could start a fire. Mary, her fingers stinging with the cold, made some strong coffee and brought a cupful to Aunt Hetty, against whose shoulder Jack had fallen asleep.

Just then there came a heavy pounding at the wood-shed door. Jack woke with a start. "What's that?" he exclaimed.

Captain Cameron hurried to the door.

Three men stood there, and a huge black dog, rising on its haunches, looked like another man.

"We've been wrecked, sir," said one of the men, who proved to be the captain; "we're from Nova Scotia, an' our schooner went ashore, about midnight, on some rocks out here."

Without waiting to hear more, Captain Cameron brought the men to the kitchen fire; and the ship-wrecked captain, a man of few words, finished his story, while Mary hurried to make more coffee.

"I did n't know where we was, but I knew it was rocks we'd struck, for we drifted right off. I could feel the schooner settlin' and I knew we could n't pump her out. so we launched a boat, though it did n't

seem much use in that livin' sea; but, in about a minute, we was flung ashore on a rocky beach place."

" You must have struck on the Hypocrites, drifted
to the southward, an' been thrown up on the bar,"
interrupted Captain Cameron.

" It was land, that's all we knew or cared," the
captain went on; " we could n't see a thing but snow,
so we crouched close together with the dog to keep
warm, an' when it grew light, it stopped snowin' an'
we saw your chimney. We 're nigh to frozen an'
famished, sir."

" Whatever we have is yours," said Captain Cameron, simply. For a moment at the door he had dared
hope one of the men might prove to be his son.

The great dog, standing on its haunches, begged
for food, thumping the floor with its tail. Jack's
laugh rang out at the droll gravity of the dog, and
his laughter seemed to break the spell of the dreadful
night.

With every helpful instinct roused, Mary and Aunt
Hetty worked quickly to give the men hot coffee and
food, and to bandage their frost-bitten hands.

For hours after, the bitter wind, though lessening
in fury, swept the cold green water about the rocks,

tearing its surface into long, glittering waves. Mary's
rowboat and Captain Cameron's dory had been washed
away; his cutter was the only boat in the cove now.

The house was almost snowed under. It took Captain Cameron the entire morning, with what help the
men could give, to make a path through the gully to
the barn. The two cows were safe, as the stout barn
had withstood the storm; so had the boathouse,
but the fishhouse on the point had fallen in.

How Mary's tired body and heart ached that night,
with the work and strain of the last forty-eight hours!
Aunt Hetty, unable to go home, was cross and irri-
table. Jack, feverishly nervous, gazed out of the window all day — his boat would be sunk deeper now
than ever. Captain Cameron, with the shovelling and
the unusual work, looked bent and aged. Their pro-
visions had been heavily taxed, and it had been trying
to have the strange men about. But Mary's courage
had not failed. At nightfall she buried her face in
the dog's soft, black fur, and felt a glow of unselfish
happiness in her heart.

When the sun burst forth the second day it brought
neither warmth nor cheer, only a clearer shaft of cold
from the deep blue sky. For another day there was

hardly a sail in sight, though occasionally a fishing vessel scudded past under bare poles; the Bangor steamboat set out late the second afternoon.

Captain Cameron's boat could not have lived in the high sea, not even to reach Ram Island. The ship-wrecked men, rough and honest, fearing to trespass on the kindness of strangers, kept themselves in the boathouse, and slept on the hay in the barn under old coverlids. They helped break the path to Aunt Hetty's house and to the well, where the salt water had to be dipped out; for the wind on that wild night carried the beach south of the house back into the marsh about eight feet, and there was a foot or more of water in the well.

The third day the wind shifted to west southwest, to stay. By nightfall a steady rain set in, reduced the snowdrifts so that the bare ground showed again, freshened the well, and best of all, beat down the sea.

The men were impatient to be off, and Captain Cameron started with them early on the fourth morning. They said good-by with awkward thanks, and the huge, gentle dog followed them slowly. With a sudden thought the captain turned, whistled the dog close to him, and asked Mary bluntly: —

" Would you like him to keep?"

"Oh, may I have him?" Mary's face was aglow in a moment.

"He's yours," answered the captain gallantly, giving the dog's head a farewell stroke; "stay with the lady, Skipper."

Just before the men started, Mary overheard them talking about sending a diver down to the wrecked schooner, but the captain dismissed the subject by saying, "There ain't a hundred dollars' worth of stuff in the old hulk, an' she's twenty fathom deep. I'll just let her go, an' get what insurance I can."

Captain Cameron brought back no letters, only a bundle of papers from Judge Weston and another package of books addressed to Mary in the distinctive handwriting.

"Boothbay folks tell me 'twas the worst storm for twenty years," the old man said; "there's been wrecks all along the coast." And this report was verified, day by day, for weeks after, by the sea's casting up on the island shores all sorts of spoil — broken oars and spars, dishes, casks of ship's biscuit, dead birds, tattered bits of sail — nothing worse, though

Mary kept away from the beaches for dread of what she might see.

Two months had passed without a word from Rob Weston. Mary had almost forgotten to count the time these last eventful weeks.

On his next trip to Boothbay, Captain Cameron carried a passenger — Mary, who was intent turning over a plan which had shaped itself in her mind.

While her father did his errands, Mary went to the Custom House, found an address in the Marine Register for a letter she had written, and then mailed the letter.

On the homeward sail she took her father into her confidence. He shook his head deprecatingly at first, but when she said, looking into his face with a tender little smile, " I know it will make him well; I *must* do it," he looked back at her with proud, loving eyes and did not object again.

Still no letter from Rob. But Mary was waiting with feverish eagerness for something else now.

It came — a letter in a cramped handwriting; and a second letter was speedily despatched to Portland.

One afternoon Jack was sitting in his accustomed place, idly turning the leaves of the new almanac.

Glancing up, his eyes as usual rested on the same spot, off Ocean Point.

"Come here, Mary," he said excitedly. "What's that tug doing out there?"

"What can it be?" exclaimed Mary, coming up behind him. She had been watching the black steam-tug for five minutes from the pantry window, with a fast beating heart.

Something was going on. Jack watched with growing interest. "What can it be?" he asked again and again, speculating and questioning, without guessing the truth. Finally, darkness cut off his view.

Then a great wonder happened. Into the cove early the next morning came that same black tug, towing a water-logged, barnacle-studded boat — none other than the *Kady*.

After the first excitement was over, Aunt Hetty called Mary into her house, and into her bedroom. She broke down and cried a bit, leaning on Mary's strong, young shoulder; then she dried her eyes with the corner of her apron, and said, "This 'll cure him, Mary. Did you see him run down to the wharf? He acts different already. Oh, Mary, how did you happen to think of doing what his own mother did n't think of?" And Mary told her.

"Did it cost a whole hundred dollars?" Aunt Hetty insisted on knowing.

"Yes," answered Mary, reluctantly.

Aunt Hetty went to the side of the bed, took out from between the feather bed and the straw mattress a long stocking of blue homespun yarn, seated herself on the bed, poured out a stream of silver dollars, bills, and small change, and began counting it.

"What are you doing, Aunt Hetty?" demanded Mary, with a singular note in her voice.

Aunt Hetty looked up. Mary had never spoken like that to her. "I'm going to pay you back, as far's I can. I'm poor, but I don't want to be beholden to anybody."

"You shall not pay me back, not a cent," said Mary in the same tone. "I owed that to Jack." She turned and went out of the room, and Aunt Hetty knew that the matter was ended.

"You planned it all yourself, Mary?" questioned Jack, coming in at noon to warm himself and to go over the story again. He had spent the entire morning hovering in ecstasy around the boat, looking her

over, handling her, even putting his fingers, with
fond tenderness, through the sail, — for, eaten by the
salt water, it gave way at a touch. "You wrote to the
diver, and made all the arrangements, and took that
hundred dollars, all you had, out of the bank! Think
of it, the men on the tug said she was standing plumb
upright, my poor boat. The diver had to take out
the ballast, and the men said it was fine to see her
come to the surface."

He stopped a moment, he was weak yet; then with
an effort he said, standing erect, his eyes gleaming
with new life, "Do you know, all the time I've felt
as though I was down there with the *Kady*, cold and
alone, and going deeper down. I can't ever thank
you enough, Mary! I must go right to work on her!"

This was reward enough. Mary cried herself to
sleep that night from sheer relief and thankfulness.

For the first — though not indeed for the last time —
something of the deeper and nobler comprehension of
human weakness and of human suffering had been
revealed to her, something of that larger knowledge
without which the sense of duty can never be fully
acquired, nor the understanding of unselfish goodness,
nor the spirit of tenderness.

CHAPTER IX.

" The Father looseth Winter's chain,
The true Creator, who doth reign
O'er Times and Seasons, doth again
Unwind the Wave-ropes that the Main
Confines within its Span."

— *Beowulf.*

" UP March hill," to the border of April, had come
the new year, begun in such great stress.
Fisherman's Island was bare of snow, and the soil,
thinly covering the rocks, had quickly dried.

All day long the sound of Jack's hammer and saw
rang out from the boathouse. The *Kady* was afloat
again, thoroughly overhauled, and as good as new;
Jack had sailed triumphantly over to see Sam Merrill
on his first trip. Now he was building a new rowboat
for Mary, — " the prettiest in all Boothbay Harbor," he
declared it should be. Every morning and every night
he ran out to the south shore and jumped a hundred
times from one shelving rock to another, for the doctor had told him it would require vigorous exercise to
overcome the tendency to muscular stiffening. He

was fast regaining elasticity of body; that of mind
had returned in one supreme flash with the *Kady*.

Mary fell again into her habit of taking long walks.
During her anxiety over Jack she had forgotten to
think so often of Rob Weston. But now that Jack
was himself again, and winter was relaxing its hold,
her mind reverted to the past and to herself. She had
only a half hope of Rob Weston's return from Europe
— a hope that grew dimmer as the days went on.

After ten weeks' silence a letter had come. She
had read it so often that the words were engraved on
her mind; but she had not answered it.

In the letter Rob told her of having changed his
studio, of feeling more at home in Paris, and liking
the routine better. And he continued: " A few weeks
ago when I was working in the Louvre, copying or
trying to copy a Botticelli madonna, who should come
along but Miss Kendall and her father. I dined with
them that night at the Continental Hotel, and of
course have seen them occasionally since; they are to
be here a month longer.

" Thank you for such a good letter. I should have
answered earlier if I had not been so busy with moving and getting settled in my new studio. I am look-

ing forward with much pleasure to hearing from you, and especially to seeing you again."

Not one definite word about coming home, — and how the mention of Miss Kendall rankled !

There was no one to whom Mary could open her heart, no one to save her from the morbid revulsion of feeling that set in. Aunt Hetty, the one woman at hand, had common ground of interest with the girl about everyday matters only ; and though there was a strong affection between them, born of good offices given and returned, their natures were totally different — the one self-sufficient, intensely practical, prosaic ; the other young, capable of generous enthusiasm and warm devotion, and feeding her mind on the noblest ideals of literature.

If there had been anybody or anything to divert the girl's mind, she would not have drifted back into depression ; for on that New Year's night the scales had fallen from her eyes, showing her to herself, wilful, unsubmissive, making a substance out of an unreality ; and there had come to her a vision of the truth that only the Infinite Love can satisfy the human heart. Later she might learn the larger truth that, in the highest sense, God's love and human love are one.

But the New Year's vision dimmed as the days lengthened. In spite of herself she clung to the old ideal ; she could no more help this passionate fidelity of temperament than the eyes she saw with. And then began that desperate struggle between courage and despair, between light and darkness, between patient submission and mad revolt, which all sensitive and generous natures must wage in their own souls at least once, perhaps many times, in their lives.

Memory at such times plays like an electric storm. Incidents long forgotten came back with singular vividness, and Mary saw the past as she had not seen it while it was the present. Remembrances of her mother, recollections of her earlier years, all the incidents relating to Rob Weston, recurred with intense clearness. And out of her contest Mary passed from girlhood into womanhood.

The early April day was heavenly fresh and full of promise. Aunt Hetty was dipping candles, —an economy she had practised since they came to Fisherman's, —and Mary, sitting in the kitchen doorway, was watching her, as one after another she dipped the already coated strings suspended from sticks, a dozen strings to a stick, into the great kettle of hot tallow on the stove.

" What ever is the matter with you, Mary?" Aunt Hetty spoke sharply. She had come of hard-working inland people, and her untiring thrift and energy were in marked contrast to Mary's more leisurely ways, inherited from sea-going ancestry. " You sit mopsin' an' mopin' round just the way girls do when they've got a beau. Mebbe you're thinkin' of that Rob Weston," she added with cruel bluntness; the storm of criticism had been gathering for some time. " Come to think of it, you have n't been the same since he went away. But *I'd* have more spunk. I would n't waste *my* time thinkin' about a man who did n't even trouble to write to me."

" If you please, I have n't answered his last letter," Mary replied with flashing eyes, her pride stung by Aunt Hetty's thrust.

" So you have been hearin' from him!" Aunt Hetty saw the disturbance in Mary's sensitive face and spoke of something else; she had scored her point. Then, because she had the girl's interest warmly at heart, before Captain Cameron started over to the harbor with fresh fish that day, she said to him : —

" Mary seems kinder ailin'. I mistrust it's because she spends too much time thinkin' about that Rob Weston."

Captain Cameron shook his head sturdily. " No, you are mistaken; Mary's too sensible a girl for that."

Seeing that she made no impression, Aunt Hetty turned homeward, commenting to herself, " What do men, pack of foolish critters that they are, know about girls, anyway?"

Unable to stay indoors, after her father went, Mary worked all day in her garden — the fenced-off square south of the house, which was a wilderness of sticks and straw and rubbish from the last year. Late in the afternoon she sat down on the porch, resting her face upon the palm of her hand.

The song sparrows twittered near her — she had fed them all through March, and they hopped around her fearlessly — the swallows darted in and out under the eaves of the boathouse, the pound of hammer and scrape of saw mingled with Jack's whistling as he worked. Curling blue smoke rose from the chimney of the little brown house across the cove — Aunt Hetty was making soap this pleasant afternoon. Across the quiet water came the calls of the Merrill children, romping around Ram Island.

Mary brushed back, with an impatient gesture, the cloud of hair which the light wind blew into her eyes. Her face was more delicate in contour than a year ago, and the exercise in her garden had brought a flush into her cheeks, grown so pale now.

The afternoon was oppressively still. Mary knew her father would not be at home until late. Everybody in her world was busy. She was too tired to work longer, and she felt wretchedly alone; even Skipper had deserted her for Jack.

She could endure it no longer. Going into the house, she threw a little red shawl over her shoulders, for the air was growing chilly, and wandered, bareheaded, toward the south shore. Wrapping the shawl closer, she sat down and leaned against a tall, mossdraped fir tree, standing close to the rocks which shelved down, tier below tier, worn smooth by centuries of waves.

The tide was nearing its full. Over on the White Island and Outer Heron the waves broke monotonously. The world might be empty of people, save for a few distant sails. The mocking ocean spread miles and miles away to the horizon, a waste of water, between her and Europe.

Aunt Hetty's words had rung in her mind all day!

Except for the noise of the water, as the long swells broke foaming, tumbling, frothing against the rocks, there was no sound.

She thought the sense of loneliness, the silence, would drive her mad.

Then the water's flinging, forceful activity riveted her attention. The waves spent their force, were splendidly shattered. Why not, like them, dash herself with all her force against those rocks? Better still, as the water slipped back from its strong upgathering, why not slip back with it?

What was life, anyway? What use was loving, what use was anything?

Her mind began traveling over the old story again. Why had she yielded to her feeling for Rob Weston? It was unworthy, without real foundation. She blamed him hotly for his unintelligible looks, his impulsive actions, his mention of home-coming, and his subsequent silence. Would it never end, this intolerable torture of memory and regret? Why not end it now?

The low, whispering wind seemed to call her, the leaping waves beckoned with foam-wreathed arms. Her brain almost reeled, for the seething water, close up to her now, was one dizzying whirl.

In despair, to save herself, she flung her arms around the tree trunk. For a moment that seemed to bend forward with her. Then it held her back.

How long she clung to it she could not tell. The tide, turning, ebbed a little with a sullen sound.

By and by she dared unloose her arms from the tree, and she tried to rise, but sank back, too weak to stand.

A sound of rushing through the dry grass, a light bound, and Skipper's cold nose was thrust in her face. A moment later Jack came running out to take his evening exercise.

"Why, Mary! What's the matter? It's long past supper time, and your father was coming into the cove just as I started. Guess you 've been asleep," he said, appearing not to notice her strained eyes, her drooping figure.

He began jumping from rock to rock, and his energy revived her. Skipper kept on licking her hands lovingly. When Jack was ready to go she summoned

strength to rise, steadying herself by putting her
hand on Skipper's head, and she held it there as the
dog walked back with her close to her side. Jack
whistled to save her from talking, and he helped her
gently over the rough places.

As her mind recovered itself in that walk homeward, Mary wondered what would have happened had
she slipped off into the water ; she shuddered to think
how near she came to it. Her father and Jack would
have walked over the island all night, calling and
looking for her, while her body was floating off with
the undertow of the tide ; and she pictured their gradually growing conviction that she had ventured too far
out on the rocks and been washed away. But her
poor old father would not have given up the search
till the last ray of hope were gone.

A bright fire was crackling in the kitchen stove, and
the teakettle was singing merrily when she entered
the house.

"Hello, my little girl!" said Captain Cameron,
depositing an armful of wood by the stove, "you're
out late. My! how cold your hands are. I'm afraid
you ain't feelin' well," he went on, looking at her
anxiously, "an' I guess you'd better have a change.

I saw Mis' Morton over to Boothbay, an' she sent pertikelar word for you to come an' make her a visit, an' have a good time. Aunt Hetty 'll look out for me all right." He had pondered over Aunt Hetty's words, found an answering echo of apprehension in his own heart, and had gone to consult Mrs. Morton, an old friend of his wife's.

Mary put her arms around her father's neck and laid her cool cheek close to his. " Let me stay with you, father. I don't care for the things other girls like; I only want to stay with you always."

And the gentle-hearted old man answered, " My daughter is so precious to me that I don't want her to go, any more than she wants to."

CHAPTER X.

"It is Nature's highest reward to a true, simple, great
soul that he thus gets to be a part of herself."
— *Thomas Carlyle.*

IN the exuberance of her sense of escape and con-
quest, Mary was merciless with herself at first,
as strong-natured young people are wont to be.
Watching her those days, Captain Cameron thought
she was growing more like her mother.

It took rare courage to begin life anew here in
this island isolation. The alternatives were simple,
loving companionship with nature — through flowers,
birds, sunsets — or a lapsing into mere negative existence given over to narrow concerns.

Instinctively Mary made the finer choice, and unconsciously she began to bind nature to herself with
fellowships which for a time quieted the need of
human association. She watched the quivering waters
curled by the breath of the morning under the deepening dawn, each day bringing a world newborn; she
opened her eyes to the glory of the sunset cloud-
worlds, and always she heard the mighty sea chanting

that mystic and eternal hymn which none may hear without awe, which no musician may learn. She fathomed countless secrets of the air and sea, countless signs of the heavens; she saw and heard and felt much of that which, though old as the heavens and the earth, is yet eternally new and eternally young with the holiness of beauty.

Slowly outside her windows the world awoke, the grass brightened, the willow buds swelled and grew, until the green and gold glory of the spring was upon the island.

Touched into harmony, Mary's nature awoke too, healed, though not satisfied quite, by the magic power of the air and the sea, whose strength seemed to enter into her. Her eyes caught anew the sea mystery, her outdoor life gave her a fresh, clear color, with sound sleep at night.

Like Mary, Jack was all alive with the spring. He had finished Mary's rowboat and was building new lobster traps to replace the winter losses.

The air was full of tender balm, and the soft lap of water on the rugged shore came in through the open south window of the best room, where Mary sat in her speak-a-bit corner, books and sewing piled high

around her, a fire burning on the hearth to dry off the
dampness of the mid-April afternoon — the winter's
storms had brought great quantities of driftwood
almost to their doors. Skipper lay stretching and
dozing before the fire. Outside, through the soft
showers, the robins called joyously.

Jack, dressed in oilskins, an old sou'easter tipped
back on his head, appeared at the open window. His
face was brown and ruddy now.

" I 've got to quit working on the new traps and go
to hauling the old ones with Uncle Charles," he said ;
"the Portland smack will be along any day now, and
we have n't got many lobsters in the cage. Come and
see us start, for luck, will you?"

Glad of an excuse to go out of doors, Mary thrust
her arms into a yellow oilskin jacket and, with Skipper
at her heels, ran down bareheaded to watch the start.

" Shall I read the last lobster law to you?" she
asked.

" We know it, never you fear," replied Jack ; " the
fish warden has n't caught us yet."

Lobstering off the Maine coast has been more and
more restricted in the last dozen years. Each doubt-
ful-sized lobster must be measured, and the "short"

ones, under ten and a half inches, dropped back into the sea, else if the fish warden happens along he can collect a fine of five dollars [1] for each delinquent lobster. The Camerons had, as usual, about a hundred traps down around the island, and "hauling the traps" meant at least two hours of hard work — mere muscular work, however, for as Jack said, "A man does n't need to know much more than a lobster does to catch him."

Captain Cameron sat in the stern of the boat, his silver-gray hair showing below his black sou'easter, a serene smile lighting his face as he turned to call good-by to Mary; Jack was speeding the boat ahead with strong strokes.

"It 'll be clear when you come back, your kelp is almost dry," cried Mary, waving the long festoon of kelp, the fisherman's barometer, which hung, a fantastic ornament, on the fish house.

Already, overhead, blue sky was showing through the clouds. Far away in the distance the sea spread itself out in sleepy stillness. A huge fishhawk splashed into the water, and Mary, watching, saw him rise with a fish in his talons and fly southward. Skipper made a jump in the air toward the bird.

[1] Law of 1897.

" I have n't seen my fishhawks to-day," said Mary, turning to follow the direction of the bird. " Come on, Skipper."

Just beyond the rocky bar stood a tall, scraggy tree, and its gnarled arms held a curious, bulky nest, to which the same birds returned each year. The great uncouth creatures had been a constant delight to Mary, for their repairs upon the old nest home had been carried on vigorously ever since their welcome coming had foretold the early spring. It was a huge nest, about three feet across and two feet deep, and it looked like a great heap of brush, dry branches and seaweed, as it was.

The fishhawks were half tame, and evidently did not mind Mary's presence. She watched them while they ate their supper, awkwardly balancing themselves on the edge of the nest, then wheeling noisily away only to return again and, after a queer nocturnal toilet, settle themselves for the night.

The sun had vanished when Mary walked back along the grassy footpath to the house, and the crimson afterglow, warm and vivid, lay over the sea. The robins were chirping good-night, a stray bluebird sang "purity, purity," and a brown thrush, rare visitor,

swelling its slender throat, sang from the willow tree
as if its heart would break. The birds had hardly
been quiet a moment all day, and Mary had worked to
their music — they seemed to her like little souls pouring themselves out in song. As there were few trees
on the island in which the birds could build, these
songsters were birds of passage, save the song sparrows.

The heavy-laden dory was rounding the point a
half mile away. Mary rekindled the fire, started the
supper, and lighted a lamp to make her father's home-
coming cheerful. The dory drew up to the lobster car,
and the two men quickly transferred the lobsters from
the dory. They did not come directly home, but rowed
across to the company's wharf, though it was darkening fast; and Mary knew they were going to catch
herring for the next day's bait, so she took a thick
wrap and went to look on, seating herself on the
wharf, Skipper beside her.

"Good luck, father?"

"Good luck, daughter; we've got risin' two hundred lobsters." That was all; fishermen at work do
not talk much.

The two men stretched the herring net, anchored it

at one end, and rowed a few rods away through the phosphorescent water flashing with fish. Of a sudden Jack turned the dory swiftly, and the fish were driven like sheep into the net, which, when they struck it, showed a long line of dull fire. Then the draught of fishes was pulled in.

"Seems to me we fisher folks can understand the Master's words better 'n most people, he taught so much by things that has to do with fishin'," said Captain Cameron meditatively, as he walked toward home with Mary in the deepening evening.

So one peaceful day followed another. And Mary felt that there was nothing more to be desired on earth.

CHAPTER XI.

"The future does not come from before to meet us, but comes streaming up from behind over our heads."
— *George Eliot.*

A LETTER lay on the table for Mary. She had just come in, flushed and glowing, from hunting over the island with her father in search of the cows, which stayed out all night now and had a trick of getting lost. Evidently Sam Merrill had been to the harbor.

It was from Mrs. Sargent, and it ran : —

" *Dear Miss Cameron,* — I have sad news for you and your father. Our old friend Judge Weston, dear, genial man, died last week, after a brief illness. I know you will grieve over this sorely, as we do, but you must try, as we are trying, to think of him as blessedly released, for he suffered intensely during his illness.

"Mr. Sargent tells me there is something in the will, just a remembrance, which concerns you. There are the usual formalities of law — the red tape has to be untied and tied again, and it will help matters greatly if you are on the spot. I have intended all winter asking you here for a visit, and now this settles it; you must come as soon as possible, for a month at least, and take more than a side glance at our old city of Boston. We will make all our lions roar for you, and I shall enjoy renewing my acquaintance with streets and statues. We will investigate that splendid Public Library and study the famous frescoes and the sweet reasonableness of those women who float in mid-air without wings or feet or any visible means of locomotion. And we will see the State houses, old and new, and hear a suffrage debate, we — in fact, we will have you see and hear it all, — Cradle of Liberty, Subway, Bunker Hill, and the symphony concert.

" I shall enjoy a visit from you, and be benefited by it, too, — young, strong, and full of savor from your island home as you are, and the children are ready to make you royally welcome.

Yours very cordially,

MARGARET E. SARGENT.

" NEWTON, April 23, 189–.

" P. S.   Tell me what day you will come, and Mr. Sargent will meet you in Boston."

Hardly had Mary finished reading her letter when Captain Cameron came in to tell her the news of Judge Weston's death, for Sam had heard it in Boothbay and had stopped in the boathouse to tell Jack.

Death had no fears for Captain Cameron; he had

faced it too often, and now it was to him but the opening of a door, the throwing off of the bodily cloak.

The father had trained his daughter to a heritage of his brave attitude, but her sobs would rise. The old man soothed her.

"It's only the pain of separation that is hard, Mary. The judge has just gone over that river where we'll all have to cross some day; but there's a sure pilot, a sure pilot, Mary," he said, smoothing back her bright hair with his knotted hand. Yet his own grief was greater, for this was a tried friend of his early days; and he was haunted, too, by the apprehension that some change might send them forth from the island home, which had been to him like a fair haven unto a weary soul.

Mrs. Sargent's invitation, it was decided in family council, must be accepted. Aunt Hetty's interest rose to an unprecedented height. "I'm goin' to buy you a new dress, a real pretty blue one, an' a hat an' some ribbons," she said, with a burst of generosity.

It required all of Mary's ingenuity to keep Aunt Hetty from purchasing the dress, and to make her content with the quiet hat Mary chose, having observed

Miss Kendall and Miss Merrick to some effect. One journey to Boothbay sufficed for the preparations, yet it was with many a misgiving that Mary packed her limited wardrobe in the small leather-covered trunk which, as Aunt Hetty said, " Your mother went on her wedding journey with."

Going to Boston for the first time was a momentous event to Mary. She told her father something of her clinging regret at leaving home, as they sat before the driftwood fire for a good-night talk, her trunk all packed.

" I should n't want you to feel any other way but sorry to leave your old father ; but partings has to be. Remember always there 's One who orders our goin's an' our comin's, an' trust yourself in his hands."

Faith in the divine comes often to our hearts through the human, and Mary rested herself in her father's words that night, sleeping soundly.

But the old man's thoughts ran on far into the night, and their tenor was this : " My little daughter, all I have in the world, is going away. Some day, soon, I shall be drifting out on the ebb tide, and what will become of her? Aunt Hetty is n't the one to satisfy

her. Dear Lord, send my boy Edwin home," he
softly prayed again and again.

There was no time to spare in the morning, for
Mary must leave Boothbay on the early boat, to connect at Bath with the Boston-bound train.

As Jack helped Mary into the boat, he thrust a small
box into her hand. "Open it when you get there,"
he said, wringing her hand in good-by.

Aunt Hetty let her breakfast dishes stand unwashed
— rare event — and sailed over to the harbor "to get
some cotton cloth for sewing these long afternoons,"
she carefully explained, unwilling to acknowledge that
she went to be company for Captain Cameron coming
back. She had promised Mary manifold times to
look out for him.

"If I was goin' to Boston I sh'd have to take a
compass to find my way round," Captain Cameron's
last words came in a cheerful voice, his face shining
with serenity.

"Be sure you take one of them parlor cars," was
Aunt Hetty's final injunction. "Folks do say things
ain't so likely to happen to you there."

It was a tender, tearful face that looked down from
the *Nahanada's* stern as the steamboat drew away

from the wharf, and the white flutter of Mary's handkerchief was visible until the boat vanished from sight behind Mouse Island.

The intricacies of the Bath station were not great, and Mary found the ride in the comfortable drawing-room car a novel experience, increasing in interest. She located the Bowdoin College buildings when the train stopped at Brunswick. Then the Flying Yankee train steamed in from up the Kennebec, and bore them off to Portland like a flash. On the way to Portsmouth she caught bewitching glimpses, across the marshes, of the familiar ocean, — which took her thoughts swiftly back to her island home, — and soon the train drew in to the Northern Union Station.

CHAPTER XII.

" Music is love in search of a word."

"'The age needs heart, 't is tired of head."
— *Sidney Lanier.*

IN a story the train would probably have run off the track, or Mr. Sargent failed to appear at the Boston station. But in real life, as a rule, trains reach their destinations, and people keep their appointments.

The tall, brown-bearded man recognized Mary in a moment, as the passengers streamed from the inward train. Almost before she knew it, they were in a cab, the trunk strapped on behind, and whirling across busy Boston. "Half a dollar extra if you make the 4.40 train at the Albany Station," Mr. Sargent said to the cabman.

Nearly every man on the Newton train was buried behind a newspaper, and a train that passed them showed a blur of white at the windows.

"Has anything special happened?" asked Mary.

" No, they always read," replied Mr. Sargent, with an amused twinkle in his eye.

"She's a restful, natural sort of girl," he had said to himself, while she was describing her journey, in her clear, low voice which had a musical turn, "and she is dressed all right, I should say," — man-fashion, noticing general effect, — "Mrs. Sargent need n't have been troubled about that."

A crowd of prosperous-looking men and well-gowned women got off at the Newton station, and greetings were exchanged as one carriage after another drove away. Mary found herself with Mr. Sargent in an open, green-cushioned carriage, drawn by a bay horse and driven by a coachman in green, bowling noiselessly past handsome houses fronted by close-cut lawns.

"There's the Eliot Church, and there is Grace Church and the new Hunnewell Clubhouse," said Mr. Sargent, pointing out the places of interest; and presently they turned into the driveway which wound up to the Sargents' house.

A white-capped, white-aproned maid opened the door, and little Katharine came dancing out — the same sweet-faced child who had sat on Judge Weston's knee listening to fairy stories at the island meeting two years before.

Mrs. Sargent was waiting in the spacious hall. " We are very glad to see you, my dear," she said, with a warm handshake; and she liked the firm grasp of Mary's hand. " You must consider yourself one of the family while you are here."

Mary felt an added sense of cordial welcome when the tall clock in the hall struck the half hour in the same drowsy tone of the old clock at home. But despite her level young head, she was glad to escape early to her room that night, for the long elaborate dinner, the brilliant lights, the opening world of new interests, were bewildering. Just before she went to bed she thought of Jack's gift, and opening the little box, found ten tightly folded five dollar bills and, written on a slip of paper, " Please get things for yourself with it."

Thursday, the day after her arrival, Mary had gone to Boston with Mrs. Sargent, and spent some of Jack's money under the older woman's supervision. To-day they had lunched in town, and now Mrs. Sargent had left Mary in her own seat, in Music Hall, to hear the Friday afternoon symphony rehearsal.

Waiting for the music to begin, Mary eagerly watched the people, as from the balcony where she sat she had her first vision of a sea of faces; and she idly wondered how many times the little house on Fisherman's Island could be set down within the hall — which seemed immensely large to her, though she was getting used to vastness now in the way of buildings.

There came a momentary hush, followed by the short *adagio* movement of a famous symphony. At first the music simply formed a background for her thoughts, as they traveled back and forth, between old scenes and new. Gradually the swelling melody took possession of her, and her soul went forth on its waves, buoyant, bending with every curve of the melody, which seemed to round and fill out her nature, to fathom all the abysses of her soul. In places it was as though little children were being rocked to sleep; again, the subdued tones seemed to shadow forth the passing of souls, then gladder sounds brought a vision of noble men and women in stately forests, where life seemed strong, and wise, and beautiful.

How the violins struggled for human utterance, as they led the great harmony, seeking, almost finding words!

Then on the bosom of soft, slow cadences she felt

herself being borne over the smooth waves of the sea, and with gladness nearing home. But the melody grew deeper, and suddenly saddened. Following, drawn along irresistibly, she trembled with emotion. Once the despair made her soul ache with dumb anguish, and the hall was blurred before her eyes; she almost cried aloud, " Oh, stop, stop! I cannot bear it!"

Turning, the melody took her as if out on a wild, stormy sea; she could hear the breakers moaning as they tumbled on the reefs, she could feel the darkness. But clear, glad, calm trumpet calls brought relief — the tumult quieted, the waves were still; it was as though all the sounds of the sea and the winds, sweet and sad, were mingled and made into one melody, and she was wafted again toward home, which lay in the golden, hazy distance. Then the music died away and left her with a great peace — but with a heartache, too, because it was more beautiful than the world.

While the people crowded out, she sat waiting for Mr. Sargent. Her rested, roused soul shone in her eyes as she looked up at the sound of an unfamiliar voice near her which was saying: —

"It was like the sea, was n't it?"

"Mr. Loring!" she exclaimed, rising to shake hands with him.

John Loring, from his seat in the balcony diagonally opposite, had readily identified Mary. He had noticed every slightest quiver of the sensitive frame, every phase of changing emotion on the open face, as her soul was being played upon by the inexorable, inexplicable power of music.

"Mrs. Sargent told me you were to visit her, so I was n't at all surprised to see you here in her place, though I should have recognized you anywhere," he said. "You are waiting for somebody; do be seated again."

"Mr. Sargent is coming for me; Mrs. Sargent does n't trust me to find my way alone," she answered, looking at him with a touch of merriment.

"May I wait with you?" He seated himself in front without waiting for an answer.

"Why did the music make you think of the sea?" she asked, after she had answered his courteous inquiries about her father. Her glance was frank and interested, and her red mouth had a happy trick of smiling.

" You know, don't you, that people who have lived by the sea, and loved it, have a two-stringed harp in their souls, and the sea-string always vibrates when it is touched, whether they will or not," he answered simply.

"Hello, John, so you've found Miss Cameron." Mr. Sargent appeared in the doorway behind them.

" Yes, and I am glad to renew the acquaintance," said Mr. Loring. " I suppose you are going out on the next train, so I'll walk across the Common with you, for I want to talk over that C. B. & Q. stock."

Mary walked between the two men, walked so well and looked so beautiful that half the people they met turned for a second look at her, of which she was wholly unconscious, for her eyes were drinking in the beauty of the afternoon, the stir of the street life, the green of the Public Garden, and the stateliness of the towering buildings.

Mr. Loring excused himself at the Columbus Avenue station, saying, " I have to go back down town."

" You will be around to see us Monday evening, I hope," said Mr. Sargent, as Mr. Loring shook hands with them both — unnecessarily, Mr. Sargent thought, but then, John was inclined to be ceremonious.

Mrs. Sargent was always at home Mondays, in the afternoons formally to the world, in the evenings informally to a few friends, who dropped in to talk, read, or have a rarebit. The Merricks, being next-door neighbors and old friends, were wont to come for the evenings, as was also John Loring.

"Hopelessly rich," men characterized Mr. Loring. This was true — with a margin — of his material possessions; but his home life was meager, for he lived in a great, old-fashioned house alone with his mother, a woman of undeviating ways, who seldom left home.

"You always wake me up here," he said once to Mrs. Sargent, half apologizing for his frequent visits.

"Come whenever you feel like it," she answered; "our latchstring is always out to you."

She was a rare type of woman. The repose, the self-reliance and command of herself, the receptive spirit that showed itself so quickly to every person she met, proved her a woman of power and resource; added to these gracious qualities were a keen intellect and a warm heart. Mr. Sargent was a lawyer in good practice, a widely-read, widely-traveled man, with a keen sense of humor and a fund of anecdotes which he related extremely well.

They talked about live subjects on those at-home evenings. To-night the conversation turned on the New England temperament. Mrs. Sargent was a Southerner by birth, and she had never become quite acclimated here.

"This New Englandism is a thing apart by itself," she declared, "and Boston seems to me a kind of national cold storage, which chills all its neighborhood. I don't go as far as some critics who say Boston people are a lot of bloodless men and unmaternal women, good pioneers, but icebergs in their homes; but I do think they would be more satisfactory if they were warmer-mannered and more self-forgetful."

"You must remember we have our traditions to keep up," said Mrs. Merrick, — she was a Colonial Dame and a Daughter of the Revolution, — "we simply can't be effusive, it's such wretchedly bad form."

Mr. Sargent took up the question. "Sentiment aside, see what New England has accomplished! The fact is, the very motive-spring here is and always has been energy."

"Yes, energy, passionate energy," put in Mr. Lor-

ing. "What else can you call the great force that
has moved this little handful of stout-hearted people
for a century, in the van of the nation? It has been
more than clear intellect and strong will which have
kept them at the head: it has been burning zeal, for
reform, and liberty, and beauty, too, — zeal untrained,
unsatisfied, I admit, but alive with intense eagerness.
It's the fighting passion of men ready to be cut to
pieces for an idea, most of all, the passion for knowledge and insight into things, material and spiritual."

Mary, listening, observed Mr. Loring closely. This
was a man who lived right in the midst of the mystery
of life.

He was tall, broad-shouldered, well-built, well-pro-
portioned, a man much given to outdoor life one could
see at a glance, though traces of indoor occupation
showed in his face, in the dark hair thinning at the
temples, and the marks of care across the high
forehead. There were good-humored lines around his
mouth, which had fine, firm curves. His face, clean-
shaven except for a black moustache, was almost
stern in repose, and showed strong determination, yet
with a distinct touch of gentleness. His eyes were
blue-gray, more gray than blue, and they darkened

almost to black when he was, as now, roused to deep feeling. They were notable eyes from their expression; the meaning of the whole face seemed to deepen in them almost to speech.

The good-humored lines around his mouth showed, as he stopped for a moment, saying, "Purpose, responsibility, you know, are my hobbies." Then he continued: "The most satisfied heart among us has to keep on working. We don't wear our hearts on our sleeves, but it's a great mistake to think our lack of expression means want of heart. If you only probe beneath the surface, you will unmistakably find the New England heart warm and deep in its personal relations. I know whereof I speak, for I am to the manner born."

"You are a New Englander of New Englanders, and cherish your limitations," said Mrs. Sargent, — her frankness was one thing that attracted people to her; "but here you can live so hopelessly near to people without ever knowing what goes on in their hearts. And you are so afraid of showing any feeling. It's in the air. Why, this very afternoon my little five-year-old Katharine was telling me the story of Moses and the bulrushes, which somebody had told her, and when she came to the part about their finding the baby, she almost cried; then she turned away, laughed, and said, 'It was awfully funny.'"

"The fact is," said Mr. Sargent, "we all take ourselves too seriously, and we load ourselves down with the woes of other people. Bear your own burdens first; after that, try to help others if you can."

"Yes," Mrs. Merrick admitted, "women are more unreasonable in this respect than men."

"Look at the average women one meets in society, at lectures, the theater, or on the streets!" continued Mr. Sargent; "their general expression of misery and the lines that furrow their faces show that they take even their pleasures sadly — as the Frenchman said. They study every art but the greatest of all, the art of being happy. If a whole generation of New England women could be born without consciences, it would be a blessing to their friends and a boon to their good looks. As matters are now, anything will serve for a really good, upright, self-sacrificing New England woman to borrow responsibility upon. But Miss Cameron looks as though she had sunk all her worries and responsibilities to the bottom of the sea."

Mary colored, as their eyes were turned to her. "Mine are different from yours," she said; "everybody here seems to have so much to do that I don't see how they find time for it all."

"We don't, that's just it," said Mrs. Sargent.

"But we have responsibilities thrust upon us." Miss Merrick had been silent before. "Here mamma is trying to have me put on as a director in the —— Convalescent Home, when I am simply staggering under clubs and societies and teas and keeping up generally."

Mrs. Merrick smiled complacently. "You are equal to it all," she said. She liked to have Mr. Loring know how capable this daughter of hers was. "Come, we must begin reading before we grow any more personal," she added; "I have brought a new book." And the rest of the evening was spent over the essays of a recent author, whose touch of romanticism had been welcomed as a relief from too much realism.

To Mary, listening rather than taking part, the whole evening seemed like a living chapter out of a book, — the handsomely furnished library, the charming gowns of the women, the sense of congenial enjoyment brought out by the conversation and the reading. She was listening, however, with unmistakable appreciation, as John Loring saw — this tall young woman, with those singularly splendid eyes looking out from beneath waving brown hair.

When Mr. Loring rose to go, after the Merricks had made a start, he said, " I believe Rob Weston is coming home on the *Campagnia* next week." His eyes were on Mary as he spoke, and to his surprise he saw a crimson color surge over her transparent face.

" Poor fellow," Mrs. Sargent was saying, " we must all be good to him for dear Judge Weston's sake."

The Sargents had three children — two sons, fourteen and twelve years old, and little Katharine. " I fairly have to keep the children away from Miss Cameron," Mrs. Sargent told her husband; " they tease her so persistently for stories about ships and wrecks and the sea." It was an orderly household, seeming to run of itself; but behind the scenes Mrs. Sargent's sure hand was on the helm. Mary reveled and expanded in the harmonious atmosphere, and she awoke gradually to a realization of the many opportunities which lie within reach of privileged woman in this Boston world. She heard good music, drove, met Mrs. Sargent's friends, went to afternoon teas, — these she enjoyed least of all, — learned to play golf, and nothing escaped her alert attention.

Thus she was introduced to the life of a society girl, and knew for the first time what it was to get up in the morning with no imperative necessity for doing one thing more than another. Social life, with the new sense of leisure and unchecked enjoyment, could hardly be without some directly stimulating effect upon her. Yet her companionship with nature and her hold on the great mysteries of life, her clear sanity of mind, as they had guarded her against the perils of seclusion, now kept her from being hurt by the sudden glimpse of the world.

Mrs. Sargent's guest speedily became a topic of discussion. She was never uninteresting ; Mrs. Sargent took care that she was suitably dressed, and she was so wholly without affectation or conceit that she won much admiration. Even Mrs. Merrick said of her, " She is fortunately possessed with the faculty of manners and making friends."

Miss Merrick had welcomed Mary with a great show of cordiality, and when Mary with scant civility in-

quired for Miss Kendall, Miss Merrick said she was
to be abroad a year, and added : "She must have seen
Mr. Weston often, because she writes so much about
him. You will enjoy meeting him again, I know."
She did not succeed in evoking any consciousness
from Mary.

CHAPTER XIII.

"Living will teach you how to live better than preacher
or book." — *Goethe.*

WITH Mrs. Sargent, Mary saw Boston's art
collections and churches and visited its his-
toric places — old as we count age in this new world.

"How I should enjoy taking her to Europe!" Mrs.
Sargent confided to John Loring. "It is positively
refreshing to come in contact with her enthusiasm,
and her good sense amounts almost to genius. Now,
some day, for the sake of teaching her to be properly
thankful, you may show her how the other half lives."

Accordingly, early one morning, Mary went to
Boston with Mr. Loring, who spent a part of each
day as social worker in connection with a well-known
social settlement at the South End. "Perhaps I
ought to have gone with them," Mrs. Sargent said to
her husband, as he was starting for town on a later
train; "but, no, it won't do any harm to give them
a chance to get better acquainted. I wonder if John
realizes he has been here every other evening this
week, on some pretext or other? And he's taken her

twice to the Brae Burn links, and once to the Country Club, for golf."

"Help them along, that's right; I used to be glad enough of a good turn," said Mr. Sargent. He remembered that a woman, though she has been married many years, likes a touch of gallantry. "But I wonder you women don't oftener run aground when it comes to steering the affairs of perverse young people."

It was but a short distance from the Albany Station in Boston to the settlement. Mary waited in the reception room, while Mr. Loring looked after a few matters of business; then he rejoined her. First he took her over the house, showing her the large living-room, homelike with its pictures, its books, rugs, and comfortable furniture, the class-rooms upstairs, the boys' workroom, and the gymnasium. "Some day I shall come here to live," he said, "for a part of each year at least, but never during my dear mother's life."

"Have you steady nerves?" he asked, as he opened the hall door. "We are going to make 'neighborhood visits,' as the settlement people call them, and we may encounter some trying scenes."

"I can hold on to my nerves, at least while I am going through things," she answered, glancing up at him with a frank smile. He stood nearly six feet tall, and there was something reassuring about his broad shoulders.

"That is a great virtue in woman, and I might have known you had it," he replied, looking down at her with a stir of admiration as she stood in the sunlight, waiting, with a happy, untroubled face, her hair gleaming, her complexion exquisitely fresh, and her air of unconsciousness.

Their first call was at a shabby little home, in a tenement over a stable. By the couch of a patient-faced girl — ill with hip disease and so small Mary could hardly believe she was ten years old — stood a table covered with a soiled red and white checked cloth, and set with an uninviting breakfast of crackers, a bit of butter, and a cup of tea. "Will you wait while I go and buy something more appetizing?" asked Mr. Loring. He seemed a different man now; he was quicker, more animated, and his eyes held a luminous look, for a great sympathy was his. In a few moments he returned with a jug of milk, a loaf of bread, and some eggs for the mother to cook.

" My man has a job to-day, the first in three weeks,"
the woman told him, her face beaming.

Mary, meanwhile, had made the acquaintance of
the little girl, who, with the trustfulness of childhood,
had put her thin hand in Mary's warm clasp. But
Mr. Loring was the older friend, and when he came
back the child gave her hand to him, and a happy
smile stole over her face as he stroked back the light,
golden hair from her forehead. There seemed something homelike to Mary about the action ; in a moment
she remembered it was her father's way.

At the next place they visited, an old mother was
caring for her son, a laboring man half sick with a
malarial, rheumatic trouble, half frenzied, too, with
grievances, real or fancied, against the rich, and
waxing so violent over the subject that Mr. Loring
deemed it best to leave after a few moments, his
errand accomplished.

" How *do* people live in such dingy, stuffy places ! "
exclaimed Mary, drawing a long breath, when they
were outside.

" That is an unsettled problem," Mr. Loring answered. " You can hardly call it living, it is only
existing. But we are working hard for better tene-

ment conditions. Our main hope to-day, though, is for the children ; if we save them, we save the nation to-morrow."

"Can you go to one other place," he asked after a moment's pause, "even more wretched?"

"Yes ; but, oh, how all this misery makes one's heart ache !" She had been thinking about the little girl incurably ill. "I should think helping this suffering would make people forget themselves and their own unhappiness," she said wistfully.

"Do you know anything about unhappiness?" he asked when he was by her side again. They were making their way along a crowded street, filled with fruit venders, swarthy-faced Jews, scurrying Chinamen, and urchins of every age. It was a directly personal question, he realized.

"I could n't have lived as I have, without knowing," she answered, thinking of the winter storms and loneliness, of Jack's wasting illness, of the island isolation — but not of Rob Weston now.

Mr. Loring felt the sadness in her voice. "It's the lot of us all, no matter where we are," he answered gently ; "but sometimes our best happiness grows out of our sorrow."

"Here we are!" he exclaimed, as he led the way into a dark little entry. "The man we are going to see is a German Jew, and he has only been in this country six months. He was n't well to begin with, and work in a sweat shop has about finished him; he is dying of consumption now. It's up four flights, so take plenty of time."

There were two small rooms, kitchen and bedroom, in the garret tenement, stifling with the hot May sun. In the kitchen three children, mere babies, were playing on the floor, and the worn little mother was bending almost double over some rough sewing. She welcomed Mr. Loring timidly, in broken English.

Within the bedroom — where there was a strange, expectant hush — on a cot bed, his head propped with pillows, lay an emaciated man, who turned his burning eyes to Mr. Loring like a hungry, hurt dog. He tried to speak, but the words died in his throat.

Mr. Loring took an orange from a bag on the table, cut it open, and began feeding it to the man, awkwardly.

"Let me do that!" Mary had her gloves off, and was by the bedside with a plate and spoon which she took from the table. She gave the man spoonful after spoonful of the orange juice, as a woman would feed a child; then, putting one arm firmly around his shoulders, she turned the pillows, and let the tired head sink back again.

"Tank you! tank you!" the sick man gasped, his deep-set eyes fixed on Mary. Then he looked toward Mr. Loring, who was standing at the foot of the bed. "Iz zee your wife?" he whispered.

Mr. Loring shook his head hurriedly. He could see no trace of consciousness in Mary's face, except that the color deserted it.

The sick man closed his eyes. "We would better go now," said Mr. Loring softly, and Mary followed him into the kitchen. He left a few instructions with some money, and the woman broke into sobs: "De doctor say he not last long."

"Have they any money?" asked Mary, when the two were down in the entry-way again.

"Only what is given them," he answered abruptly, "and this is but one of hundreds of cases."

"How can God let such things be!" she exclaimed passionately.

Mr. Loring met her protest with silence, but his heart smote him when they were out in the daylight

again, and he saw the anguish of pity on her face. A
swift recollection came to him: it was this pity, this
sympathy, of which he had dreamed.

Half to himself, half to the woman now at his side,
he said, " If each of us bore the burden of helping
those in need, whose lives touch our own, it would go
a long way toward solving the problem. The world is
waking up at last to the truth that humanity is greater
than temples and all the theories taught in temples."
Then he said, contritely, for her face was still pity-
ingly set, " I ought n't to have brought you to this last
place — though I had to come myself this morning."

" I am glad you did," she said, turning her shining
eyes to him.

" This is enough for to-day, I am sure; " he spoke
very gently. " Now I will take you to Mr. Sargent's
office to settle that long delayed business."

Mr. Sargent's law office, on School Street, was
musty with books and papers. Two long papers,
ready for signature, lay open on a table beside the
desk, and Mr. Sargent gave the brief explanation, —
that Judge Weston had left his five shares of stock,
representing half of the island property, to Mary, and
had expressed the wish that the entire island might

come into her possession some day; and thereupon the other owners had agreed to make over their shares to her, for they felt that future visits to the island would mean nothing without Judge Weston's presence. Here was the letter, signed by them all.

"Is it mine? Am I to own the island?" Bewildered, Mary looked from one man to the other. "Judge Weston and the owners have given it to me? Then we need n't ever go away!"

John Loring turned and stared out of the window. Mr. Sargent drew up a chair for Mary, and busied himself with pens and ink. "I could hardly help telling her that John had bought those shares in from the other owners," he confided to his wife afterwards.

"There, Miss Cameron, please sign your name here. Read the paper first, though; a woman should n't ever sign anything without doing that. Now, John, you witness the signature."

The ink was thick and black, and the two signatures on each paper seemed to stare up at Mary.

"I shall have to ask you to take Miss Cameron to the station," said Mr. Sargent, folding the long documents, "for I have an immediate engagement. You have just about time enough to get the 12.10 train."

Tremont Street was crowded as they went along toward the Common. They did not talk much, even when they emerged into the greater freedom of the Common, but there was a restful sense of understanding between them.

"Do all Boston women carry bags?" Mary asked once; she had counted thirty in the crowd passing one block.

As they walked under the tall elms toward Park Square, John Loring was thinking, half-unconsciously, of the school-mistress and that long walk which the Autocrat wrote about. Mary, while noticing the old men and little boys along the side paths, was puzzling over something in the background of her thoughts.

Mr. Loring left her at the station, explaining that he must go back to the settlement. On the way out to Newton a light broke upon Mary's mind, and at luncheon that noon, after they had talked over the island ownership and all it meant, Mary said to Mrs. Sargent, "It wasn't you who sent the papers and books to me all the year, was it?"

"What makes you think not?" asked Mrs. Sargent, fencing a little.

"Because the writing on the wrapping-paper was

the same as Mr. Loring's when he signed the deeds,"
answered Mary, directly. " Did he send everything?"

" Yes," acknowledged Mrs. Sargent, cornered. She
expected Mary to pursue the subject, but Mary remained silent, an inscrutable expression in her eyes.
So Mrs. Sargent went on, after a moment: " I read
your letters to him, and he really had your thanks."

Another pause; then she continued: " There are
many interesting things about John Loring. His
father was a banker, a very wealthy man, and until
he died, about five years ago, John, who was the only
child, was with him in the Boston office. John keeps
the office now, and has a clerk there to look after his
property, but he gets out of business more and more,
and just gives himself up to social reform work. He
comes pretty near to being a saint — or a martyr — in
his relations with his mother, for she is an exacting, no-
tional woman, not very well, and naturally devoted to
him. Years ago, — let me see, we came to Newton
seven years ago, and it was about then, — John had
some great disappointment over a girl who must have
played fast and loose with him, for as the story has
been told me, they were engaged a year, when she
suddenly married another man supposed to be

richer. People say John had almost worshipped her
— though they always say such things. But evidently
the disappointment did n't turn him into a misanthrope
or a woman hater; he simply grows more and more
devoted to his social work, until I am sometimes afraid
he will become a hopeless fanatic. He spoke about
his past once, only once, to Mr. Sargent when they
were off together somewhere, — of course Mr. Sargent
told me, — and said he never should marry. He's
a young man yet, only thirty-three, and it's dreary
for him, I know, although he never says a word
about it or makes any complaint. But many a
man envies him, and many a girl would like to be
Mrs. John Loring."

"That's a long chapter," she concluded, "and it
sounds like gossip." Perhaps it was unnecessary,
but she had felt she ought to tell this to Mary. "He
is always doing helpful things, and last summer, when
you told us what you had been reading, and I spoke
of sending you some books, he remembered it and
sent them himself; and when I showed him your first
letter, he simply said he would rather the books
seemed to come from me; so I lent myself to the
harmless deception. It is a small matter, and I

would n't speak about it to him, if I were you," said Mrs. Sargent, as she rose from the table.

Mary was looking down at little Katharine, who had left her place and come to Mary's side; it was comforting to have the child near her.

There was a debate on the woman suffrage question that evening at the Hunnewell Clubhouse. "Even if we have to give up the Dog Show, we must let Miss Cameron have a taste of the suffrage, or her Boston experiences will not be complete," Mrs. Sargent insisted when her husband demurred, at dinner, to attending the meeting.

Carriageful after carriageful of people was deposited at the entrance to the handsome colonial building, for the suffrage question continues to be a live issue.

A gentle-faced, sweet-voiced woman was the first speaker, and she pleaded warmly for the suffrage right. Then the opposing side was taken by a thin-voiced. inadequately equipped man, who scored a few points and said effusive things about women; "they rule us now, and it's too bad to accumulate too much power on one side," was his final argument. Next a frothy, aggressive-mannered young woman delivered a fierce tirade about the success of woman's work to-day, and the therefore-to-be-claimed success of the suffrage privilege if exerted by them. Last of all, a fine-faced woman, full of years and dignity, spoke briefly, making a final point that "one woman, simply by being her own womanly self, has more influence for good and more power for reform than ten women clamoring for the ballot."

Mr. Loring joined the Sargent's party, as the audience broke up into groups after the discussion. "How do you feel on the subject?" He spoke to Mary.

"I suppose the suffrage is sure to come, sometime, but I don't want it for myself," she answered in her straightforward way. "I don't know much about it, though of course I have read the papers; it seems to me that women ought to attend to what concerns them most, and I don't believe voting is the most important thing."

"I think you are right. If women would turn their attention to what lies in their power, near them — just as I was saying this morning — that would bring the social millennium sooner than anything else."

"Why do people here have so many societies and clubs and lectures?" She asked the question in all sincerity; it had been a puzzle and surprise to her.

"The fact is," he answered, with the smile that made his face so winning, " men and women in this modern Athens — the women perhaps more than the men — are warmly interested in progress and reforms. There's a good and an unfortunate side to it; and there are so many organizations of the kind that they might well be classed under a general head of 'Societies for Putting Things to Rights.' It is the tendency of the times."

"But why not leave off talking so much, and just live?" she asked, a touch of merriment in her brown eyes.

"That is rank heresy!" he replied, with an answering flash of fun. " You will be sent forth as a Philistine if you venture such comments. How would you have people live?"

"Oh, out of doors more, with the birds and the flowers," she answered.

"Most girls wouldn't find that very exciting," he said, looking at her attentively.

"It doesn't always satisfy me," she answered frankly, "yet I've felt stifled here sometimes, it's so — so — civilized!"

She looked more as though she belonged outdoors than in, as she stood there — with that indefinable

outdoor atmosphere, tall, firm-figured, in her simple
dark blue street suit and white silk shirt waist, her
beautiful hair shining under the blue straw hat, un-
trimmed save for some ribbon and quills; she wore
her clothes well, her most severe critic had to admit
that.

She was woman enough to know that Mr. Loring
was attracted toward her. His manner had not lost
the animation of the morning, and his eyes were full
of kindly interest. Mary hardly allowed herself to
meet them; Mrs. Sargent's story had been constantly
in her mind, and there was a restraint about her manner which had not existed that morning, — the sense
of content in his presence was broken in upon by a
growing embarrassment. She was relieved when Mrs.
Merrick and her daughter came toward them.

After a few casual remarks, Miss Merrick said to
Mary, "Did you know Mr. Weston arrived in New
York yesterday? He called this afternoon."

The unexpected mention of Rob Weston brought
an added constraint to Mary, and meeting Mr. Loring's eyes just then, she colored deeply, wave after
wave flushing her face. But the Merricks did not
notice her embarrassment, for at that moment Mr.

and Mrs. Sargent, saying good-night to the people they had been talking with, turned at the mention of Rob's name.

"He has really arrived, has he?" asked Mr. Sargent. "I wonder he did n't come around to my office to-day."

"I must look him up early to-morrow," said Mr. Loring in a steady voice, his eyes still on Mary.

"It 's insufferably warm here," Mrs. Sargent interrupted, noticing Mary's flushed face, "and as we have talked the suffrage subject threadbare again, we may as well go home."

"Won't you ride home with us, John?" she asked; he had walked to the door with them.

Mr. Loring shook hands with Mary after he had declined Mrs. Sargent's invitation. "Is it day after to-morrow that you start for home?"

"Yes."

"I am sorry," was all he said; but he looked at her with such strange, bewildering intensity that the color did not leave her face until they reached home, nor the sense of his pressure on her hand.

That night John Loring, turning back, as was his wont, to those days which, though seven years past now, had never seemed more remote than yesterday, was startled to find in the place of the old ideal a vision of clear, shining eyes, a recollection of sweet voice and compassionate, womanly presence. Hour after hour he paced the floor, while the gradual reconciliation went on; then, like the sane man he was, he accepted the fact, nay, he welcomed it, and his hope went toward it.

But why had the mention of Rob Weston so visibly affected her, twice? He had told her he was sorry she was going home, but in his heart he was glad, now that Rob had come.

And that night Mary, wide-eyed, wakeful, went over the manifold events of the day — the morning sights of misery and sharp anguish, her new ownership of the island, the lunch-time talk with Mrs. Sargent, the evening occurrences. She remembered that Rob Weston had come home; but what did it mean that in place of thinking about him she was wondering over the meaning of Mr. Loring's look? Then the merciless story of his life came back again, and with all the strength born of past overcoming, she resolutely laid her hand on this ecstatic, vital thing which was springing up in her soul.

CHAPTER XIV.

"Love is not love
Which alters when it alteration finds,
Or bends with the remover to remove."
— Shakespeare.

"I grieve not with the moaning wind,
As if a loss befell;
Before me, even as behind,
God is, and all is well."
— John G. Whittier.

MARY did not open the book, but let it fall on her knees, while her eyes wandered to the library window, where, looking down across the sloping lawn, she could see the sunshine falling on the rich clumps of spring flowers and, beyond, the sleeping hills. The fragrant air came in through the open window, and a golden oriole was calling with liquid note from the larch tree. The air indoors seemed heavy, so after a moment she went out on the broad veranda. She had dressed early for dinner and was waiting.

Two letters had lain by her place at breakfast that morning. One, several days old before its start, was from Aunt Hetty, who had written, "Don't let city

notions turn your head. Your father says, stay till
you are ready to come home; he is getting along all
right, though I expect he misses you a sight. I suppose the summer visitors will be as thick as potato
bugs along the shore when you get home." The other
was a brief note from Rob Weston, saying he especially wanted to see her and would call about five
o'clock.

Mary seated herself in a corner of the veranda,
partly sheltered by climbing vines; it would be easier
to see Rob out of doors, after all.

Coming up the driveway in a cab, Rob saw her,
and walked around the house to her unannounced —
the same impetuous, self-confident Rob, his face
browned by the sea voyage, his blue eyes touched
with grief for his uncle. There was evidently a strong
nervous tension about him, and his greeting was
constrained.

"Miss Merrick tells me you are going home to-
morrow," he said, as he sat down opposite Mary on
the low bench which bordered the veranda. How
beautiful she was in that white India-stuff gown with
its bit of lace — it was an old-fashioned gown, re-
modeled from one that had been her mother's.

After a few restless remarks about her visit and his voyage, he began twisting his hat nervously in his hands.

" Why did n't you answer my last letter? "

" I hardly thought you cared to hear from me."

" Why not? "

" Because you were so long about writing."

" But you see, I was working like a dog, and there is n't much a fellow can write about, and I did n't know definitely about coming home."

He stopped. She said nothing, but looked away. He forgot for the moment certain passages of flirtation with Miss Kendall.

" And I could n't ask you to marry me, as I can now."

She was still silent, but an inward protest rose unfalteringly.

" Did n't you know last summer that I cared for you? "

"Sometimes I thought perhaps you did."

" Then why are you so different now? "

" Because — I don't know. It was a long, hard winter, and things seem different."

He grew more eager as she appeared to elude him;

moving nearer, he bent forward and tried to take her hand. But she withdrew hers, and the pleading in his eyes was lost upon her, for her own were downcast.

Rob rose and walked restlessly back and forth, cursing his folly for waiting, and recalling rapidly those days last summer.

" Why did you ask me if I had ever been confirmed ? "

" Because I thought I cared for you ; because " — the womanhood in her rose, and truth compelled her — " I did care in an imaginative, unreal way, and I thought then that coming into the church, in itself, was the gateway to heaven ; and, oh, it was childish, but I thought I should feel better about your going so far away if I knew I should see you again." Her face had grown very pale and gentle; she seemed to be speaking of some one other than herself.

The man's better nature was touched, and he saw, as by a revelation, the change which had been wrought in less than a year, transforming the immature girl into a woman infinitely more attractive. " That is enough to make a man try to win heaven," he said softly, seating himself opposite her again. Then after a moment, " There must have been something real in your feeling. Why can't you learn to care for me again?"

No yielding in her face, only a growing, infinite pity.

"Miss Mary," he said hotly, roused again, "if you won't marry me, how can I believe in goodness, or heaven, or anything else? You will kill my faith."

"Mr. Weston, this is unworthy of you; it is n't manly." She drew herself up in her chair, her dark eyes showing darker by contrast with her white face. "When a woman confesses to you that her feeling for you was only imaginary, only a girl's fancy, built on trifles, have n't you the manhood to accept it?"

"They were not trifles; I loved you all the time," he said bitterly, "fool that I was not to tell her so then," he added to himself.

His eyes traveled from her to the distant hills. "Think how Uncle Levi would have liked to have us care for each other," he said, looking at her again. He saw the sudden weakening at the corners of the firm mouth, and his hope awoke. But Mary was thinking of Judge Weston's words, " Be true to yourself."

"Is there any reason why you can't try to care for me?" he asked, with a desperate determination to have a definite answer.

There was one quick leap of her heart, which Mary thrust back as she answered " No."

" Then will you try? Let me ask you again this summer. Give me this chance," he pleaded.

" My answer will be just the same then," she replied wearily. " I am sure of this, Mr. Weston." She turned her beautiful, steady eyes full on him now; and he, looking into them, saw that she spoke the truth. But he clung to the hope.

" At least give me the chance," he insisted; " it will help me to be a better man. Promise me you will try."

She hesitated. It was weak not to hold to her " no." But it might help him, and a woman's heart is always tender toward a man who has confessed his love for her.

" I promise," she said, and with that he had to go content.

About nine o'clock that evening Mary was upstairs, while Mrs. Sargent's maid helped pack her trunk for the morrow's start, when Mr. Loring called. He asked first for Mrs. Sargent, and he found her in the library. She saw that he had something especial to say to her, so she chatted on until he was ready. His face was noticeably pale, his absorption unusual. After a few moments — he had heard nothing of what Mrs. Sargent said — he began : —

" You know the history of my life — an unfortunate only child, having too much kindness and too much restriction, growing up self-willed, and then blindly starving my life because I could n't have what I wanted? I have waked up at last — I have had to. Do you know why? "

" Yes," she answered simply.

" Is it — would you advise me to try now? "

" Oh, John ! " she exclaimed, reaching out her hand in sympathy, " I am afraid it 's too late. If you had only asked me yesterday ! There is something between her and Rob Weston, for he was here this afternoon, and just as he was going, I was down in the library and they were on the veranda, and I could n't help hearing her promise him something."

Mrs. Sargent was startled by the look of anguish in the man's eyes. For a moment he kept her kind, steadying hand, then rising and looking down into the fire before which they had both been seated — it was a raw, chilly evening — he said, in a voice full of suppressed emotion : —

" I should like to see her to say good-by."

Mary was reluctant to go down, but Mrs. Sargent urged it, saying, " Remember how much he has done for you." So she went, and Mrs. Sargent stayed behind, looking out from the hall window into the dark overhanging night, murmuring, "Poor John! poor man ! "

Downstairs Mary found him standing by the fireside in the library — it was just where Mrs. Sargent had left him. He looked up and came forward as Mary entered the room.

The graceful, clinging white gown made her look taller, more womanly, than ever. Her hair, disarranged with the work of packing, was loosened around her face, her brown eyes shone out like stars, and there was a tremulous smile on the sweet red lips.

"I will keep you only a moment," he said, "because it is growing late and you ought to be resting for your journey." His eyes were drinking in every detail of her face.

" Have you heard from the German Jew to-day?" she asked, lifting her eyes.

" I was there this morning ; he died at noon."

" Is there anything I could do — send them a little

money or anything? I have some left that was given me to spend."

"I'm afraid not," he answered, a gleam of pleasure lighting his face and his eyes shining with that bewildering look, under which her own eyes fell again.

With a visible effort she broke the impending silence. "Mrs. Sargent told me, or rather, I found out from your handwriting on the deeds, that it was you who sent all those books to me, and I want to thank you for them."

"It was a very slight thing to do," he answered, putting aside her thanks.

"Slight to you, probably, but it meant a great deal to me in those long winter days."

"I shall be glad to send more"; he could surely let himself do this.

They had both remained standing.

"Why, oh, why, did he come to torture me again?" Mary was saying to herself.

Not daring to trust himself longer, he took her hand in his for one mute moment, looked strainingly at the downcast face, and without saying good-by, went out into the night.

Mary was standing by the dressing table, absently

looking down at the candles, when Mrs. Sargent entered in response to Mary's low " Come in " after her
knock.   She wanted to have a farewell talk with her
guest.

" I am sorry you feel that you can't stay longer,
but you must surely come to us for a good visit next
winter.   We shall probably see you before then,
though, for Mr. Sargent has decided to buy a yacht,
and we shall go cruising along the Maine coast this
summer."

Mary's face was still preoccupied ; she had seated
herself opposite Mrs. Sargent, but was only half listening.

With a natural curiosity, Mrs. Sargent was speculating on the exact relation between Mary and Rob.   She
ventured : —

" I wish you might marry and live near Boston
some day.   You surely can't think of staying on that
island always."

" How is a woman to know when she loves a man
enough to marry him?" came the unexpected question.
" What is love, anyway?"

" Oh, it 's a kind of ' inward unaccountability and
an outward all-overness,' as a brother of mine used

to say. It is n't easy to define, just as is true of all high and noble things."

"She stopped, then, seeing the trouble in the girl's face, she went on : —

"Marriage increases one's enjoyment and appreciation, it doubles all there was before, if the love is true and deep. But don't ever marry anybody you can live without, anybody whose mere presence does n't satisfy your heart, whether he brings you peace or not, whether he is a scamp or a reprobate or an archangel! Love does n't necessarily bring peace. That greatest lover of all who ever came into the world said he came not to bring peace but a sword. If you want peace, go into a convent. Love brings satisfaction, but never entire peace."

Mary's face was full of unrest; she was thinking, "If only I could tell it all to her," but the words would not come.

Mrs. Sargent yearned to help her; there was something she had not fathomed. "Perhaps separation is the best test of love," she said, rising, and tenderly putting her hand in passing on the bright hair. "Wait a moment, I am going to read something to you." She vanished and reappeared in a moment,

settling herself with soft rustlings of her silk bedroom gown in a large chair near the dressing table.
"A happy, happy woman!" thought Mary, looking
at the fair-faced woman as she began to read, first
saying, "This is something I came across the other
day in the *North American Review*, and it refers to
that natural looking forward to marriage which every
true-natured woman ought to feel."

"If this eagerness for marriage arose from desire
for sympathy, and if constant efforts were made to
render their minds more intelligent and graceful, that
they may be able to keep some rare love in a husband,
and that they may train, in all beauteous mode, his
children, we should not quarrel with them. There are
men possessing high minds and souls of delicate sen-
sibility, hungering to find in woman what a fate that
they do not, dare not doubt, tells them is in her; are
hungering to form some real marriage; and they roam
the world's garden, where the flowers are arranged in
choicest order, saying in sad disappointment, 'They
do not answer us, speak to us, are no companions,
have so little love, are *not* true women.' "

"Dear, there *are* men in the world like that," said
Mrs. Sargent, holding Mary for a moment in a good-
night embrace, "and I hope you will know it some day."

After Mrs. Sargent went, Mary sat for a long time with her head upon her folded arms. Eleven chiming from the great hall clock reminded her that she would be starting in less than nine hours now. She was utterly glad to be going home, and the only desire that possessed her was to be alone again.

The east wind moaned at the window. Mary finished her packing, put out the candles, and went to bed in that state of dumb submission which knows, though it cannot feel, the reality of the Everlasting Arms underneath all events.

CHAPTER XV.

" Ay, so the gods send us
The darkening cloud, that we the radiant bow
In twice triumphant brightness shall behold! "
                            — *Brunhild.*

DONALD CAMERON was at home when Mary arrived, — her Uncle Donald, back from his South American voyages. His old-fashioned face, lined with the furrows worn by a life of exposure, his figure bent with rheumatism and hard work, past his three score years, he was about ready to come to anchor for the rest of his life.

" I 'll make one more trip, then I 'm goin' to turn the *Flying Kestrel* over to my first mate," he announced the evening after Mary's arrival, when they all came together for a family conference. He " set great store by Mary," as he said, and had waited her return to announce his news. " The shippin' business ain't what it used to be," he went on sententiously, " for steamboats an' railroads have cut freights down to almost nothin'. I 've saved 'bout enough, with what I 'll have comin' in from the schooner, to keep me an' Hetty the rest of our lives. Jack, he 'd better stick to boat buildin'."

It had never been his plan to have Jack follow the sea. "No, goin' to sea's the last thing I 'd let a boy o' mine do; there ain't nothin' I know of that 'll send him straight to perdition any quicker. It's a dog's life, too, nowadays." He was a bluff, outspoken man, uneasy on land, like all seafarers, and especially ill-content on Fisherman's Island.

"If I 'm goin' to be dry-docked the rest o' my life, Hetty, it's got to be somewheres else 'n this place." He always came home from sea with a bold front, and this time he kept it up. "Why, the first thing I 'd know, I 'd be walkin' round this tarnation place, an' go straight off into the water. You 'd have me an old barnacl'd wreck on your hands in no time."

So the news that the island property had come to Mary, while it kindled afresh their affection and respect for Judge Weston, served but to increase the perplexities of the two families.

"If Donald won't stay, I can't go an' leave Mary an' her father here all alone," Aunt Hetty reiterated helplessly, divided against herself.

"Well, well, I can settle things better after I 've

slep' over 'em," said Captain Cameron ; " let 's drop
it now." He did not want Mary's first evening at
home spoiled by a long discussion with Aunt Hetty.

" Mebbe we 'd better shut the houses up an' all go
over to the main to live, I guess," she said to Mary
one day, rehearsing the situation for the hundredth
time. " Your father seemed to me kinder failin' like
last winter, an' I 'm thinkin' it 'd be pretty tough
gettin' through another winter here."

" But what would father and I have to live on?"
asked Mary.

" I 'll take care of you, Mary," put in Jack, " just
as long as I can build boats."

" Jack 's very partial to Mary. If they was n't
cousins, I expect they 'd like each other well enough
to fix it up between 'em," Aunt Hetty confided to her
husband. She occasionally surprised herself, and him,
too, by talking things over confidentially with him.
In her heart, she was dryly thankful he was going to
give up the sea ; but nothing would have induced her
to tell him so.

Their difficulties were settled, however, speedily,
and in a manner they little anticipated.

Eighteen years old when he ran away from home,

Edwin Cameron — Mary's brother — had not found making his way in the world an easy path. He had shipped on a fishing schooner, as his father rightly conjectured; but there were forty or more of these vessels bound from Boothbay for the Banks at that time, and when Captain Cameron came out from the rage which drove his son away, these vessels had been twenty-four hours at sea. From the George's Banks to Portland, then on an English steamship to Liverpool, had been Edwin Cameron's course. The wretched ill-treatment he experienced at sea, latterly a stirring fascination about the great city, kept him in Liverpool. Sore with a sullen sense of grievance he had vowed never to return until he was a man independent of his father. Working first around the great Liverpool docks, obliged to live anywhere, cut off from home ties and home tenderness, his indomitable perseverance and inherent integrity alone enabled him to rise, in spite of circumstances. At the end of ten years he reached a breathing place; next in line of promotion to junior member in the large shipping firm of Laking, Hatton & Vincent, he was now in a position of comparative ease, and he resolved to go home. He had intended writing, years ago, after his anger wore away; but this he kept putting off, telling himself he would soon go in person. At last the impulse grew unconquerable, and sailing from Liverpool, he arrived in New York the last of June, and quickly made his way to Boothbay.

No one in his native town recognized him. "There's Donald Cameron goin' by now," the old shopkeeper said, pointing out of the window with his forefinger as he finished his account, in which the foreign-looking man had appeared greatly interested, of the Camerons' removal to Fisherman's Island. The visitor hastily left the shop, and the old man, watching the meeting outside, was mystified by the surprise on Donald Cameron's face, and the evident constraint of the stranger.

Donald Cameron, sailing back to the island in the *Kady* that afternoon, — he had been off all day house-hunting,—brought a passenger, eager-eyed and nervous.

"Son, I knew you would come home some day," said the old father, as after the solemn, thankful pause which followed their meeting, he stood with one hand on the shoulder of the tall, resolute-faced man; "an' I knew you by your boy's look, the first minute."

But when the father would have humbled himself

for his part in that tragedy of the past, the son would not allow it. "The past is past, father, let us say no more about it," he protested, after his explanation of the years that lay between; and the father saw that the subject was too painful for many words.

It happened often during those next days, as he saw his son in and around the house, a broad-shouldered, full-grown man now, prop to his old age and protector for Mary, that the father wiped furtive tears from his eyes; the strain of so much happiness made him tremulous.

Mary, eleven years old at the time her brother went away, had slight memory of him. "So you are really my brother?" she often repeated; and her quaint gravity over him was very winning to the man, who, remembering his mother far better than the little girl, found in his newly acquired sister so great a likeness to the mother — whose death was the one grief now which time had not canceled — that he could hardly do enough for her. As a sister and as a woman she answered his expectation. "Gad!" he said to himself, "some day I'll have her come and keep house for me, but not in that beastly, smoky Liverpool."

He could be absent only a mouth, which left little

more than a week to arrange for the comfort of his father and Mary. Accustomed as he was to rapid action and quick decision, two visits to Boothbay sufficed for the purchase of a large house, capable of adaptation to two families. " I've set some men at work to get the house into good shape," he said, telling them of his purchase, " so it will be quite ready for you early in the fall."

On the morning before he left, he put a checkbook into his father's hands. " Here is something for you to draw on freely, for you and Mary, in the Boothbay Bank ; draw to any extent, there 'll be more to come."

The old man looked steadfastly into the honest blue eyes, so like his own, when he bade his son good-by. " I 've sailed from New York, from Philedelphy, an' Baltimore, an' New Orleans, an' Liverpool, an' Barcelony, an' almost every other port on the globe ; I 've never amounted to anythin', an' I 'm glad I did n't either. Yet I 've had my compensations. The Lord's mercy has been sure an' unfailin'. He brings us all home to the truth, sooner or later. His givin' you back to me is the one thing I 've prayed for most. Now I 'm ready to go home, — home to your mother, whose heart I nigh to broke. God bless you, God bless you, my boy, my boy!" said the white-haired man, putting his hands in benediction upon the head bowed to receive it.

"You'll welcome me home many a time yet," said the son, when he could control his choking voice. But this was not to be.

When Edwin started for New York, Donald Cameron went as far as Boston to take command, for the last time, of the *Flying Kestrel*, and the two families settled down to spending the remainder of the summer on the island, — though Jack was often in Boothbay, superintending the building of a boat shop, to have ready in the autumn.

Aunt Hetty apparently had a new lease of life; there was a manifest struggle going on within her, which Mary, gifted with the saving grace of humor, watched with keen interest. Either her loneliness during Mary's absence, her husband's decision to settle down at home, or their bettered circumstances — perhaps all three combined — was responsible for Aunt Hetty's growing anxiety to be conciliatory, which so visibly warred against her critical self-righteous tendency, — her stone of stumbling and rock of offense. In the midst of a sharp sentence she would stop suddenly and shut her mouth with a snap. "I declare for it," she broke out one day, attempting to laugh at herself, "I shall bite my tongue off, the first thing I know."

"I s'pose you did n't get a beau while you 's gone," Aunt Hetty ventured one dull afternoon, — they had ample time now to talk over Mary's visit. "Seems to me you 're gettin' to be somethin' of an old maid. But then, mebbe there 'll be chances for you over to Boothbay next winter."

Mary bent lower over her sewing, and Aunt Hetty went on with the monologue.

"After all, though, if a woman 's fairly well off, an' comfortable, I say she 'd better not get married. She gives herself up too much. She 's got a master then, an' she 's got to do what he wants her to; mebbe he don't say it in so many words, but there 's looks that she sees, if nobody else don't. An' when she wants to go away, it 's ' No, don't go; I shall be lonesome!' I tell you, when a woman 's married, she 's got a master, an' she ain't the same as she was before. But land sakes! men *are* masterful, anyway. I suppose the Lord made 'em so. Just see how your brother went to work an' bought that house, an' just see how set your uncle was not to stay here next winter." Secretly, Aunt Hetty liked her husband all the better for his insistence.

Back from the busy town life with its spirit of the present, to the simple life of nature, touched with the mysterious sense of the to-be, Mary had taken up the humble routine of her daily cares with that steadfast adjustment which is the heritage of a well-balanced mind. The unusual events in the home life immediately after her return helped her through the transition, and gave her nature a chance to react from the strain of those last days in Newton.

She wandered over the island like a bird, examining her flowers, watching the fishhawks, drinking in the glory of dawns and sunsets, and of the blue sea. How she had learned to love the barren little island! Yet how pitiably limited life was here!

This June weather brought such longing days — days when all the unrest of her nature awoke and thrust forth a claim for recognition, days when she tried to persuade herself into caring for Rob Weston. Marrying him would mean escape from the monotony and narrowness of this passive existence which pressed upon her more heavily now that she had tasted the charm of congenial companionship and breathed the larger breath of life; but in her heart she felt this would be doing him cruel injustice.

Rob Weston wrote twice during the week after her return, passionate, pleading letters, and the second one she answered. The next letter she did not answer; its wild insistence almost terrified her. Then no more came for several weeks.

Strongly as were her thoughts drawn toward John Loring, as strongly she fought the feeling. "What right have I to believe he gives me a thought beyond that of simple kindness?" she pitilessly rebuked herself again and again. Yet back of all her resolution, in her inner consciousness, his influence was upon her life.

A half-divine, half-maddening discontent kept her out of doors working around her flowers, walking, or spending long hours on the rocks, reading, — a package of books, Stevenson, Kipling, Burroughs, and several magazines had arrived for her not long after she reached home, — reading, while the unresting ocean came lingeringly against the rocks at her feet, and the fearless sandpipers flitted by, their soft gray colors blending with the pebbles and the rocks. And living thus, she felt the dream-realization of a world of activity and beauty and love, made up of vague, mingled images from the books she had read and the experiences, real and imaginary, shadowed forth in her mind.

Outwardly her life went on much as ever in the old routine. More tender with her father, more patient with Aunt Hetty, she fought her battles out alone. There was nothing else for her than submission, save stark rebellion — and how could one rebel on a lonely island in the midst of the sea! Life was just dreary, that was all. "Will it be this way forever?" she asked herself passionately.

She began to count the time until they should go to live on the mainland. At least she could forget herself there in some kind of activity — anything would be better than these uneventful, interminable, maddening days.

CHAPTER XVI.

"To ease another's heartache is to forget one's own."
— *Abraham Lincoln.*

DON'T you think I can get out by to-morrow?" Rob Weston turned wearily on the couch and looked toward John Loring, who was writing at a desk in the upstairs library — a man's room furnished with simplicity and good taste.

"Can't tell yet, Rob," Loring answered, looking at his patient critically. "The fever seems to come back every night, even now." Then he raised the window shade, straightened the rug over Rob's feet, and resumed his writing. At last he laid aside his pen; it was too dark to see any longer and too warm to have the gas lighted.

For more than three weeks Rob Weston had been under John Loring's roof, ill with an attack of malarial fever, which was aggravated by an exhausted system and mental despondency. Loring had found him playing billiards one day at the University Club, with flushed cheeks, feverish eyes, and hot hands; and he had peremptorily taken him home, none too soon, for during the first ten days Rob showed such depression that the doctor forbade his being left alone.

All the more because his own life was dreary, his heart bitterly sore, John Loring, stilling his own rebellion, had lavished unremitting care upon Rob. It was his vicarious offering to Mary Cameron. Only that morning Rob had written to her; John himself had mailed the letter at Rob's request.

"You've been good to me, John." Rob's voice broke the stillness of the darkening room. "It was almost a case of ' a stranger and you took me in.'" Another pause. "Do you mind if I talk about my own affairs a while?"

"Surely not. Go on." The ready answer did not lack any tone of sympathy.

"It's about Miss Cameron," said Rob; the hopeless note in his voice filled John Loring with surprise. Then after a moment he related the whole story straight through.

Rob, having previously gained everything he had tried for, had taken his defeat hard.

"Has she positively told you she could never care for you?" John Loring's heart seemed to stop beating as he waited for the answer.

"Yes, told me so and written me so," said Rob, with a groan. "It's no use hoping, I saw that in her face that day; she was only trying to be generous when she gave me that half chance. There's no use in my going to see her, so I've got to be man enough to give her up and take myself back to Europe to work as soon as I can. I wrote her so this morning."

A long silence fell between the two men; and John Loring was as thankful as a woman for the darkness. Presently, in a voice which soothed Rob unconsciously, he led him on to talk of his work, — Rob's genuine love for it was unmistakable, — till he found his patient growing absent-minded and excited again.

The older man lighted the gas, mixed a quieting drink and gave it to Rob, then helped him off the couch into the adjoining bedroom, after Mrs. Loring, a shadowy, gray-haired old lady, had come in for a moment to say good-night.

When Rob had fallen asleep, John Loring left the house and quickly walked the half mile that lay between his own home and the Sargents'.

"Does your invitation still hold good for that yachting trip in August?" he asked Mrs. Sargent, who was sitting on the veranda. "I find I can go with you after all, unless you have asked somebody else." He stood expectant before her.

" Yes, it does for the sail as far as Bar Harbor; but unfortunately we have asked the Merricks to come back with us from there. We shall be delighted to have you go, if you think the one voyage is worth while."

" Worth while! I should say so, to a man who has been stifled with the heat all summer." He gave an excited laugh.

" Remember we expect to start about the fourth of August. Stop a moment longer, can't you? Mr. Sargent will be at home from the club soon."

" No, thank you. I must go back and see if my patient is asleep for the night."

" You look pale and thin, John," Mrs. Sargent said, with real concern, as the light from the library window fell upon his face when he turned to go. " You have been kinder to Rob Weston than he deserves, I believe."

" No, none too kind, I assure you. Good-night! " he said, abruptly leaving her.

" What has happened to make John Loring change his mind, I wonder?" queried Mrs. Sargent of her husband.

" Above all things, don't ask him," he answered.

" Henry Sargent, do you need to say a thing like that to me after you have lived with me fifteen years?" she demanded.

Rob was asleep, and John Loring sat until late into the night looking upon the sensitive face, boyish almost, as he lay there asleep; and if the face lacked somewhat of firmness, it was compensated for, the older man thought, by the nameless charm that lay in its symmetry and beauty of feature. " I should think any woman could love him," he said to himself. " Will it happen that his loss is my gain?"

The next two weeks dragged on leaden wings to John Loring. The springs of his life ran in deep places, and these springs had been deeply stirred. Night and day Mary Cameron's face haunted him, and to be with her again seemed the one good in all the world.

CHAPTER XVII.

" Love took up the harp of life."
— *Alfred Tennyson.*

WHEN Mrs. Sargent wrote, later, to tell Mary that they would probably reach Fisherman's Island about the seventh of August on Mr. Sargent's new yacht, the *Atlanta*, she hesitated, and finally did not add that Mr. Loring would be with them.

The swift-sailing yacht came to anchor in the island cove a day earlier than the Camerons, calculating the average run from Boston, had expected; but southwest winds had sped her swiftly along, and she was a record-breaking yacht, with a spoon bow, long overhang, carrying, beside her mainsail, two jibs and a gaff topsail. She was about seventy feet long over all, and had a good cabin with plenty of room aft.

All these details Jack, from the boathouse, was taking in as the *Atlanta* anchored. Seeing the sailors preparing to lower the tender for the party to land, he ran like the wind out to the south shore, where Mary was reading, with Skipper lying at her feet.

" The Sargents have come in a stunning clipper of

a yacht. Hurry! She's a regular up to date flyer," he exclaimed, and off he ran again.

When Mary came around the corner of the house, flushed with the haste, her hair tossed by the wind, the huge black dog bounding at her side, she found Mr. and Mrs. Sargent sitting on the front porch, and, to her amazement, Mr. Loring with them.

Mrs. Sargent began explaining. "You see, we could just as well bring Mr. Loring with us as not, and he needed the voyage." She had adjusted many things to her own satisfaction when she learned, immediately after John Loring's change of plan, that Rob Weston had engaged passage for Europe and was not going to Maine before he sailed. She liked John Loring's straightforward action; there was no half-heartedness about his attitude. "That will go a long way with a nature like Mary Cameron's, whatever her feeling is," she told her husband, whose slower masculine comprehension had at last grasped the situation.

Mary's hand had barely touched Mr. Loring's in greeting. An unconquerable shyness made her move away from him and try to escape his attention.

Aunt Hetty and Captain Cameron soon appeared to give their welcome — the one from the little brown cottage, having stopped to put on her best dress, the other from the island hilltop, where he had been picking raspberries.

Aunt Hetty's attempts at hospitality fitted her about as smoothly as her best black cashmere gown.

"We was n't expectin' you so soon, so of course you did n't find us ready," she said apologetically. "I don't see how we 're goin' to make you comfortable, Mis' Sargent."

"Oh, please don't trouble at all about us. We shall be here only a short time, and we shall live right on the yacht," replied Mrs. Sargent, turning to Captain Cameron, whose delight over the guests was unbounded. With the dignity that never deserted him, he said : —

"I 'm sure I 'm glad to see you. You gave my little girl such a good time this spring as she never had before," and he put his hand on Mary's shoulder. She had drawn near him, and as she now stood by him, before her friends, she felt John Loring's glance upon her, bringing the rich color anew to her face.

It was the same sweet face under the gleaming hair ; but the eyes had lost something of the content he had first noted in Newton ; there was a suggestion,

too, of dependence on her father as she stood there
by his side, — less of the unconscious self-reliance
she had shown before.

"We will have an early supper on the boat, and
then come up and sit on your porch through the
twilight," Mrs. Sargent was saying; she feared their
unexpected arrival might have disconcerted Mary.
"Come, too, Mary, — I shall call you Mary, now.
We are going to cruise up the Sheepscot River to-
morrow, and you must go with us for the day.'

"Oh, thank you, I should like to go, but—"; the
girl was plainly embarrassed.

"No 'buts'! We have n't sailed all the way from
Boston to see you, only to have you disappoint us.
We start with you at nine o'clock to-morrow morning,
sharp, to catch the tide," said Mr. Sargent.

"Of course you 're going, Mary," put in Aunt
Hetty; "there ain't a thing to keep you home."

Overruled as to the yachting, Mary begged off from
the supper. "I shall need the time," she insisted,
"if I am going to be away to-morrow."

"Why, oh, why, has he come? I cannot bear it!"
Mary cried to herself, in the brief interval she had
alone. All her staunch resolution had deserted her;

she felt weak and unnerved. The touch of his hand, the sight of his face, with its pallor, which the yachting voyage had failed to remove, roused her into the knowledge that she must fight the battle through again. She dared not, must not give way now, for the Sargents were her friends, and they had come to see her. But it was with a heavy heart that she met them again after supper.

"What beautiful flowers!" exclaimed Mrs. Sargent, as she caught sight of the little garden full of summer fragrance, — for Mary's care had been rewarded with an abundance of blossoms, brilliant and fragrant.

"Come here, Margaret, quick!" Mr. Sargent called to his wife from the porch. Down by the boathouse, in the midst of encircling white wings, the old captain stood feeding innumerable white gulls. Tame and fearless they hovered around, almost taking the food from his hands; and he, standing among them, seemed like a shepherd with his sheep, — only for a moment, though, as, startled by Mrs. Sargent's moving nearer, the gulls vanished in a whirring cloud.

"So you live here with flowers and birds," said Mr. Loring to Mary, walking up to her.

"May we go in to see your 'speak-a-bit' corner that you told me about?" asked Mrs. Sargent. And moving away quickly from Mr. Loring, Mary led the way into the house.

The best room was full of spicy wood fragrance mingled with the sea atmosphere — that salt, savory odor, distinctly tangible.

"Such priceless things as you have here!" cried Mrs. Sargent, examining the tables, the china, and the ornaments, with the delight of a connoisseur. Aunt Hetty, in the background, listened with swelling pride.

"What is this? — my curiosity conquers me," asked Mrs. Sargent, stepping in front of an inlaid tip-table.

"Oh, nothin' much," answered Captain Cameron, opening the mahogany case and showing an instrument on its worn velvet lining. "That's my sextant, the only one of my sea instruments left, old an' rusty like myself, now."

John Loring's eyes lingered over every detail of the room; here, as Mary told them, was where she spent much of her time. He saw the books he had sent her filling the bookcase Jack had built into her corner. He picked up one lying on the table

near by. It was a copy of Tennyson, and where
the book opened in his hand he saw underlined the
words : —

> " A man more pure and bold and just
> Was never born into the earth,"

and at the side, written in Mary's hand, "This is my
father." He closed the book, reverently.

The perfume of the mignonette stole around the
house as they sat on the porch in the twilight. The
night was perfectly calm, silent, and filled with a
transparent haze ; the sea was moving only because
the tide lifted it.

"Stars are a kind of bread an' butter that never
fails the sailor," said Captain Cameron. The Sargents
were leaving the conversation to him, and he had been
spinning sea yarns ; he had just ended one with
"I tell you, it's a sublime sight to see a full-rigged
clipper ship, specially on a dark night, with the
wind whistlin' through her shrouds, when mebbe the
men have to go aloft on the yards to take in the
sails, with the ship drivin' ahead into the blackness, an' all the water showin' those phosphorescent
items."

"I don't understand how you could settle down

here after your stirring life, Captain Cameron," said
Mr. Sargent.

"Well, you see, sir," answered the old man,
after a moment's thought. "It ain't life itself in
lonely places that's the matter; it's the way people feel toward each other that makes 'em happy or
miserable wherever they are. Sometimes I get beat,
I admit, when the weather's bad for a long spell
or the lobster traps are specially hard to haul; but
then I always go back to David an' his Psalms. No
one ever had a harder time than he did. I expect
livin' out here's come hardest on my little girl," he
added.

"I've been happy enough with you, father," came
Mary's low voice in the darkness. She was sitting in
the chair next to him, and no one saw her slip her
hand into his; that worn, hard hand seemed to hush
the tumult in her heart.

John Loring was leaning against the ridge of rock
close to the porch, not far from Mary; she could feel
how near.

"Those dear, drowsy crickets are positively sending
me to sleep," said Mrs. Sargent, breaking the silence
that had fallen over them all. "Life on the ocean

wave, anyway, is the best sleeping potion I know. It must be time we went back to the yacht."

There was a little more talk about to-morrow's plans, then Mary and her father walked down to the wharf to see the guests into the tender. John Loring had counted, for the last half hour, that she would give him her hand when she said good-night; but she eluded him. The evening had brought meager satisfaction to him; instead, he felt a gnawing anxiety lest his coming was in vain, she had shown so little gladness to see him, had indeed so plainly avoided him.

The seventh of August dawned, a rare, golden day. A rush of pure joy in living, of fulness of feeling, swept over John Loring, — something of the old childlike feeling of fearless trust that comes back to us, with the richness of mature experience between. "I must have faith in what other days, if not this day, will bring forth," he said, reassuring himself.

The morning sunshine lay bright on the sparkling water, the air was strongly salt and stimulating, when the party gathered for the start. Mary, up since daybreak, after a restless night, had gained a little fresh courage with the day; but there was a tension about her that suggested the undergoing of a trying ordeal, rather than the beginning of a day of pleasure. She wore her dark blue dress, with its coat, a white shirt waist, and a white sailor hat; Mrs. Sargent's glance swept over her with approval.

" It's a splendid day for a sail," said Captain Cameron, waiting on the wharf to see the *Atlanta* start; " the wind'll be with you all the way up the river, an' you'll have the tide comin' back."

Moved by an irresistible impulse, Aunt Hetty kissed Mary good-by. Watching now from the kitchen window to see the last of the *Atlanta*, she suddenly put her apron over her eyes. " What an old fool I am!" she said; " but I s'pose everybody was young once."

Back in the north lay Boothbay, its wide harbor filled with white-winged yachts and dingy, picturesque coasters. In the southwest Squirrel Island showed gay with bright-painted cottages. Over in the east the Ocean Point colony basked in the sunlight, while here and there busy steamboats plied about, laden with summer travelers, and many schooners, bound for the Banks, like gulls were skimming over the water on long tacks, now half-concealed in its troughs, now tossed on the tops of the billows.

"Better go out round Cape Newagen an' into the Sheepscot," said Captain Cameron, when the *Atlanta's* sailing master had asked his advice; "you'll never have a better chance, tho' it's a 'reef tops'l' breeze."

The wind, against the tide when they started, blew up a heavy sea, and when they reached the Cuckolds' rocks, they were running under reefed mainsail; even then, to keep the boat up they had to ease the sheet until the luff bagged five or six feet.

"Going around Cape Newagen means a rough passage, with a wind like this," said Mary. "Do you mind it?" she asked, for Mrs. Sargent was growing pale.

"Mind it! I'm a wretched sailor except before the wind," replied Mrs. Sargent. "I must go below and lie down," she added, disappearing.

Mary's eyes had kindled with the stir of the *Atlanta's* rush through the water; the wind and the motion disturbed her not a whit, but a feeling of dismay seized her. She had hardly spoken to Mr. Loring thus far that morning; now, the sense of Mrs. Sargent's presence lost, she avoided as much as a look in his direction.

They were dashing through the waves, leaving behind them a long trail of sparkling foam. Out at sea was a wide sweep of blue, reaching far to the open ocean, which lay rolling, tossing, and breaking into white caps under the bright sunshine.

"You must have a warmer wrap, Miss Cameron." Mr. Loring brought his steamer-rug to her as he spoke. Her face was aglow with excitement.

"No, I don't need it," she protested.

But he proceeded to fold the rug over her shoulders. A stray tress of her gold-brown hair blew across his coat sleeve. She had never looked more winning.

"Thank you," she said coldly, "I really don't need the wrap." But she could not help a thrill of pleasure at being taken care of in this strong, manly fashion.

"Is she shy or just indifferent?" he asked himself as he walked away and seated himself on the deck of the cabin, sore puzzled to account for her coolness.

His position gave Mary a chance to observe him more closely than she had before done. He looked younger in his knickerbockers and short rough blue coat than she had thought him in Newton; but his face had not worn that look of care, nor the sense of defeat which it now showed in repose, as he sat there looking eastward toward Fisherman's Island, vanishing in the distance. Her heart smote her vaguely as she saw the sadness in his expression; the sympathetic element is never far absent from the heart of a woman.

"What's that steamboat off there to the southward?" asked Mr. Sargent of the man at the wheel. "One of the White Squadron, yes," he said, answering his own question as he looked through the marine glasses. "They're ahead of time, too, and that means we will have to go on to Bar Harbor to-morrow, Miss Cameron, I'm sorry to say."

Mary turned abruptly, as if to brush the hair away from her face, when Mr. Sargent began consulting the sailing-master about tides and courses. "Only one day out of a whole summer of days!" she said to herself, passionately. The day which had looked interminable at the outset, now all at once seemed to be but a fleeting moment.

John Loring gave the White Squadron scant welcome in his thoughts. He had counted on two or three days' cruising, at the least, in the vicinity of Fisherman's Island. "Only to-day, and she is so strange, so remote! Dare I risk it? Can I wait?" he asked himself.

They had rounded Cape Newagen, with its picturesque fishing settlement. Heading up the river, they met the flood tide, and the master soon had the *Atlanta* under full sail as she ran before the wind, passing the Southport shores and Hendrick's Head light. The motion grew easier and up opposite Ebenecook Harbor, Mrs. Sargent appeared in the companion-way, pale yet, but triumphant.

"We are in smoother water, I know," she said. "What! 'way around the Cape and I have n't seen it! Never mind, what is scenery without the capacity to enjoy it!"

"We 've got the wind abaft the beam now, ma'am," said the sailing master; "no more heavy seas to-day."

"Did I hear you speaking of the Squadron?" asked Mrs. Sargent, seating herself by the side of Mary, and taking the girl's firm, browned hand into hers. "I wish you could go to Bar Harbor with us."

"Yes, we sighted one of the steamships," answered Mr. Sargent, "and we 'll have to make for Mt. Desert to-morrow; we almost ought to start to-night on account of possible fogs."

Mrs. Sargent felt the hand within her own tighten convulsively.

"To-night? not to-night, surely," said Mr. Loring, with a quick glance at Mrs. Sargent.

"We will see about it later," Mrs. Sargent replied. "A dozen parties and receptions are n't to be put in the balance with a day like this on the Sheepscot River. Mary," — the girl, who had been looking straight in front of her, out to sea, turned toward her — "your aunt came down to the wharf this morning, and we had a good visit together. She says she shall be glad enough to go back to Boothbay."

"Yes, Aunt Hetty enjoys people," said Mary, absently.

"She told me some interesting things about you and Jack. Evidently the sun rises and sets, in her eyes, for you both. She said you both had been brought up to feel no fear, or at least, if you feel it, not to show it. I liked that."

Was there any meaning back of Mrs. Sargent's words? Mary wondered. At all events they roused her. "What is there to be afraid of, ever?" she said, a sudden gleam of her old happy smile lighting her face.

" Your aunt told me, too, about the accident Jack
had last winter, and how you had the *Kady* raised for
him," Mrs. Sargent went on. " Why did n't you tell
me about it? "

" I did n't think it was worth telling you," she
said ; but then and there Mrs. Sargent went over the
whole story, which had lost nothing from Aunt Hetty's
relating.

" Mrs. Sargent, you are making too much of it," at
last Mary interrupted in self-defense.

" No, I 'm not ; but I will spare you further confusion. Still, perhaps women always exaggerate in
their stories ; men say we do."

" I wish you had heard your aunt talking about
Jack, and seen her as she straightened herself and
snapped her eyes ! " exclaimed Mrs. Sargent after a
moment. " ' It is n't that I 'm proud of him,' she
said, ' because I believe when you 're proud of things
you have them taken away ; but I 'm pleased. Jack
has n't so much school learning as some, but he can
row a boat and shoot a gun and stand up straight and
tell the truth.' "

" Pretty good recommendation for a young man,"
said Mr. Sargent, heartily. " He looks it, too."

After that they fell to talking of the scenes along the way, as the river, narrowing, brought them nearer to the shores. Fresh odors from the fields mingled with the saltness of the air, and the cloudless sky revealed that tenderness which no painter or poet can ever re-image.

On the *Atlanta* bore them, past McCarthy's Cove, past the mouth of the Cross River, past Fowle's Point and "the Indian," that myth figure on the rocks of the Westport shore, up to Edgecomb Eddy and the Sheepscot Narrows, where the fortified government blockhouse, dating back to 1812, stands guard on Davis Island — enchanted island, with its dreamy, delicious woods; and high noon found them just beyond the Narrows, where the river widens out into the noble harbor at Wiscasset.

"Dear old Wiscasset and its long bridge!" exclaimed Mrs. Sargent; "what good times we have had here, Henry," she added.

"Yes, that long bridge could tell many a tale," he answered. "The old town has romance and history enough to make a dozen books."

"Was n't it here that Miss Howard wrote 'One Summer'?" asked Mr. Loring.

"Yes," answered Mrs. Sargent; "only Edgecomb was Wiscasset, and Wiscasset Edgecomb in her story."

"We will come here next year for more than a look," said Mr. Sargent; "but now we must turn about if we want to get down the river before nightfall."

Seizing an opportunity, John Loring drew Mrs. Sargent aside after dinner, which they had the steward serve on deck. "For heaven's sake, don't start for Bar Harbor to-night," he said in a low voice; "though I don't know that it matters!"

"Trust me," she answered. Then she added, "Trust yourself John, too."

The strong, beautiful day wore on. The afternoon sun bathed everything with warmth, yet the delicious sea breeze tempered the heat. All the air was slumbrous with the minute music of insect life. There was less wind than in the morning, but the sailing-master took advantage of all there was, and the *Atlanta* made good headway.

"Probably Miss Cameron does n't want to have this fragrant air spoiled by your cigar smoke," said Mrs. Sargent after a while, with a significant glance at her husband; "come out to the bow with me for your smoke — I am going out there to read." And she walked away, expecting him to follow.

But Mr. Sargent was too comfortable to leave the cushioned stern, and as Mary quickly said, " Oh, no, I like the cigar smoke, do stay here," he remained, for he was already dozing.

" I found Sidney Lanier's poems in the cabin," said Mr. Loring, coming up to Mary ; he had been wandering restlessly over the yacht, and this was the first time he had deliberately approached her since the rug episode in the morning. " Would you care to have me read aloud? We seem to be left very much to our own devices."

" I wish you would read," she answered, turning her eyes upon him momentarily ; she had been giving herself up by degrees to the dangerous delight of the day.

He threw aside his yachting cap ; the awning was sufficient protection from the sun. Yes, he was thinner, his temples showed it ; and Mary's heart smote her again. " How hard he works ! " she thought.

All men of the finer fiber feel the relation between themselves and nature, the contact with something more than is seen, the divine immanence. John

Loring felt this relation, this suggestiveness, vividly. Opening the book, he began reading in deep, rich tones, which gave back the echo of his soul, the marvelous " Sunrise " poem.

Once he let his eyes wander off over the fields and hills. " Think what the freedom of this country here would mean to people in hot, crowded city streets to-day, especially the children, with never a breath of fresh air!" he said; then he turned to the book again.

As he read, glancing at her from time to time, he saw that the music of the poem brought into her eyes the same rested, roused expression he had seen that day at the symphony concert.

" Do you want to hear a song sparrow that belongs right where you are reading? Listen!" she said, as a child might.

Together they listened. No other sound than the pure cadence of the bird disturbed the echoless air; the place and the day had found a voice.

From the "Sunrise" poem John Loring turned to "The Marshes of Glynn." Mary followed the reading closely, the beautiful word images stamping themselves on her mind.

> "—good out of infinite pain,
> And sight out of blindness,—"

he repeated, stopping the reading there.

The air and the regular sound of John Loring's voice had sent Mr. Sargent off to sleep. But there was the sailing-master at the wheel.

Mr. Loring moved and seated himself opposite the man, who was well behind Mary. She looked up, expecting him to go on reading. As she met his eyes, her own eyes were held by a look that seemed to penetrate to the depths of her soul.

Just then Mr. Sargent stirred and roused himself, saying, " I must have been taking forty winks."

John Loring muttered something beneath his breath and went forward, where he remained talking with Mrs. Sargent. When they came aft again, Mrs. Sargent said : —

" I am sure we would better stay at anchor to-night and get an early start to-morrow, Henry. I 'm not a good sailor, you know, and you don't want to take a dragged-out woman to the Bar Harbor festivities."

" This is better than parties," assented Mr. Sargent lazily. " How about the wind to-morrow?" he asked the sailing-master.

"Oh, it may haul round a few p'ints to the west-'ard," answered the man, his round blue eyes on Mrs. Sargent—he saw that she was averse to starting. "This is the kind o' wind that dies out at night, sir, so we would n't make much headway if we was to start, an' there ain't a mite of fog anywheres."

"That settles it," said Mrs. Sargent promptly. "How stupid, anyway, to go back to good clothes and ceremony after this informal existence!"

"You knew all about Bar Harbor beforehand," remonstrated Mr. Sargent. "For my part, I like isolation."

"So do I—with somebody in it," she replied.

Then they fell to talking about books, and from books to travel. "Books are good, but they don't take the place of people and travel for inspiration in living," was Mrs. Sargent's dismissal of the subject.

"How much longer are the Kendalls to be abroad?" asked Mr. Sargent.

"Until December. I suppose they will see Rob Weston again in Paris," answered Mrs. Sargent.

Mary's face did not change a whit under John Loring's watchful glance. She kept away from him yet, but she had lost the sense of dread and fear; it was impossible to hold them, after that look, that revelation of one soul to the other. Come what might, she had this precious day for her own, always.

The Sargents reminiscenced long over Italy, where they had spent a year of their early married life; and Mary, who knew many a story of foreign countries from her father, told them in that low voice which was music to John Loring's ears.

Five o'clock found the *Atlanta* plowing her way through the back passage out into the waters of Mouse Island and Boothbay. Steamboats and pleasure parties in the many catboats that cruise hereabouts saluted the handsome, swift-sailing yacht as she passed, and the *Atlanta* dipped her pennant in reply.

"Let's have supper out of the way before we come to anchor, then we can go up to see the sunset from the top of Fisherman's," said Mrs. Sargent, as the slant shadows told of the closing day. "Miss Cameron was regretting last evening that we had n't gone, for she says the outlook is glorious."

Supper was a farce to John Loring, and to Mary likewise. One thought was in the mind of each — the day, the perfect day, was almost over. John Loring's eyes were dark with intensity of feeling.   He did not succeed in meeting her eyes.

They reached Fisherman's Island before six o'clock; and this time the *Atlanta* came up to the wharf, for the sailing-master had learned the bearings of the cove.

"I must go home and look after father first," said Mary, once landed.   It was Mr. Sargent who helped her out, spite of John Loring's intent.

"May I walk over to the house with you?" asked Mr. Loring.

"Thank you," she said.   "Skipper is here to meet me."   "Why is she so blind?" thought Mrs. Sargent.

"Come back so we can start in half an hour," she called out, as Mary walked away, one hand on the dog's head.

Captain Cameron was off somewhere in his dory; Mary had seen this at a glance when they sailed into the cove.

Once inside the house she threw herself on the bed in her own room.   The swift reaction from the day's tension overcame her.   Away from them all, away from him, she felt the slight thread of happiness spun in the golden afternoon slip from her grasp.   Was this love, this mysterious relation to another soul? Could she see him again? But she must, and the moments were going!

She rose and went to the open window, letting the cool air blow on her face. It would be only a few hours longer, then this would go out of her life again.

How bitterly cruel it all was! Why did God let it come to her? Was God a father, if when his children asked bread, they received only a stone? "My own father would be kinder!" she exclaimed. Had he ever refused or withheld anything he thought she ought to have? Could God be less kind? Blindly her faith groped back, led by the thought of the gentle old man whose own faith was almost lost in sight. She tried to pray, but the words would not come.

Was it in answer to her wish to pray that a sudden recollection came to her? When they had entered the house last evening, her father, divining her agitation, had lifted her face toward him.

"Something is troubling my daughter," he said, and she had answered, "Father, can you always trust the will of God?"

"Always." How clear his voice had sounded. "My only fear is that I shall let my own will conflict with it."

Skipper had followed her into the room. She felt his rough tongue gently licking her hand.

"Dear Skipper," she cried, throwing her arms around the dog's neck; "we must go now."

She brushed back her rumpled hair, removed the traces of the hot tears that had started, steadied herself with her hand on the door before she left the house, then walked, bareheaded, toward the wharf.

John Loring watched her approach, fear and hope contending in his heart. Against those somber gray rocks, coming along that footpath, was where he had first seen her, at that first annual meeting of the owners — tall and lithe then as now, but now with the softening grace of womanhood about her. There was something untamed and fearless in her bearing; communion with nature had set an indelible trace upon her. She was unlike other women, for it is only in solitude that strong natures grow up in their own way; and Mary had grown into womanhood in one of the solitary places of the earth.

Aware that the traces of her emotion showed in her face, Mary carried herself yet the more bravely, one hand buried in the dog's black fur. As she stopped in front of them, Mrs. Sargent held out her hand.

"My courage fails me," she said; she was leaning against a post on the wharf, vigorously applying her smelling-salts. "I have a wretched, dizzy headache, so you will have to excuse me from seeing the sunset with you. But the rest of you go, just the same."

"I can't stand that stiff climb!" exclaimed Mr. Sargent, glancing up at the steep hillside in apparent dismay. "Sitting around boats all day is hard work for a man used to his comfortable office chair."

"We may as well give up going," said Mary, in an indifferent voice; "it will be almost as beautiful here." She was standing like a statue; her hard-won self-control steadied her.

"But we don't get any view here; I want to see the sunset from the hilltop," urged Mr. Loring, with uncompromising insistence.

"You young people can climb hills better than Mr. Sargent and I can," said Mrs. Sargent, "we will wait here for you. Go, Mary," she added; "it will be a positive charity to put a view such as you say it is into the mind of a tired man who declares that he must go back to his work next week."

Mary turned to Jack; he was looking the *Atlanta* over with a critical eye. "Come with us, Jack."

But Jack was deaf to the mingled entreaty and command in her voice. Boats were even dearer than Mary. "I can see the sunset any time. The sailing-master's going to draw a model of the yacht for me; he says the *Kady's* got some first-rate lines," answered the all-absorbed Jack.

There was no escape. "Why should I be afraid," thought Mary proudly. "It will only take a few minutes," she said, with a glance at the sun which was sinking fast.

Turning, she walked ahead up the path. Skipper started to follow, stopped after a few rods, then walked back toward the house. Mary did not miss him, but she heard John Loring's sure step close behind her.

She refused his proffered help from one rocky point to another.

Seeing her mood, he did not offer to assist her again, though the way was steep and rough.

He had brought his steamer rug, and this he spread on the summit rock for her, seating himself a few feet away.

Slowly the sun sank into the cloudless west, and the purple light fell on sea and land.

Burnt Island and Ram Island lights had flashed out when the sun went down, Seguin, too, Pemaquid, and Monhegan, miles away at sea; she told them to him, one by one, with never a look at him.

The stars throbbed forth in the heavens, and the glory began dimming in the west; the night opened its heart, and the splendor of the eternities drew all about them.

A dreaming bird called to its mate. No other sound disturbed the echoless air, and the silence fell like music on their souls.

"I must go now," Mary said, rising and breaking the silence.

"You liked what I read to you this afternoon?" he asked, rising too. His eyes were turned seaward.

"Yes"; her voice shook a little.

"There is another poem I wanted to read to you, not from Lanier, but something I have always liked. This is part of it," and he began: —

> "We two stood there with never a third,
>   But each by each, as each knew well;
> The sights we saw and the sounds we heard,
>   The lights and the shades made up a spell
> Till the trouble grew and stirred."

He waited a moment. "Shall I go on?" he asked, turning his eyes to her. She met his look.

"Oh, the little more, and how much it is!"

but the rest of the verse remained unquoted, for that look drew them together.

There is a moment when souls know all, without that one should utter a word.